# A Gathering of Flowers from Shakespeare

GERARD BRENDER À BRANDIS

# A Gathering of Flowers from Shakespeare

with Quotations Selected and Interpreted by

F. DAVID HOENIGER

The Porcupine's Quill

Library and Archives Canada Cataloguing in Publication

Brender à Brandis, G., 1942–
A gathering of flowers from Shakespeare / wood engravings by Gerard Brender à Brandis and quotations from Shakespeare selected and interpreted by F. David Hoeniger.

ISBN-13: 978-0-88984-290-8
ISBN-10: 0-88984-290-6

1. Brender à Brandis, G., 1942–. 2. Flowers in art.
3. Shakespeare, William, 1564–1616 — Knowledge — Botany.
4. Flowers in literature.
I. Hoeniger, F. David II. Shakespeare, William, 1564–1616 III. Title.

NE1113.5.B72A4 2006 822.3'3 C2006-900212-6



2 3 4 •

Published by The Porcupine's Quill, 68 Main St, Erin, Ontario NOB 1TO.
http://www.sentex.net/~pql

Copy edited by Doris Cowan.



Represented in Canada by the Literary Press Group.
Trade orders are available from University of Toronto Press.

We acknowledge the support of the Ontario Arts Council and the Canada Council for the Arts for our publishing program. The financial support of the Government of Canada through the Book Publishing Industry Development Program is also gratefully acknowledged. Thanks, also, to the Government of Ontario through the Ontario Media Development Corporation's Ontario Book Initiative.

Canada Council for the Arts
Conseil des Arts du Canada

Canada

ONTARIO ARTS COUNCIL
CONSEIL DES ARTS DE L'ONTARIO

I know a bank where the wild thyme blows,
Where oxlip and the nodding violet grows,
Quite over-canopied with luscious woodbine,
With sweet musk-roses and with eglantine.
There sleeps Titania sometime of the night,
Lull'd in these flowers with dances and delight.

— William Shakespeare, *A Midsummer Night's Dream*

# Introduction

Though not a botanist, Shakespeare as a poet and dramatist wrote many memorable lines about flowering plants. These have inspired artists over the ages, to whose works we hope the engravings in this book will be a worthy addition.

Shakespeare, like Chaucer before him, and Keats and Shelley and Whitman long after, had a special fondness for flowers. The unusually keen and wide observation of life that marks the characterization and human drama in his plays also informs some of his more vivid descriptions of plants and their habitat, as several passages in this book show. Yet this does not mean that Shakespeare studied plants like the keen naturalist or gardener who is interested in the clear distinction of related species. Often he was content with a mere family name, like violet or lily or pink, and therefore, unless the context provides some other clue, the engravings accompanying such passages show what we think was the most familiar species of the family in England in Shakespeare's time, either in gardens or in the wild.

Of the three kinds of gardens at the time, medicinal herb, fruit and vegetable, and ornamental, the two latter especially were being constantly enriched by interbreeding (see Perdita's speech on page 58) and by importation from other parts of the world. But as a man from a small country town, Shakespeare also knew the common flowers of fields, wastelands, woods, heaths, and marshland (see, for instance, pages 108 to 117). Many members of his audiences in London too — a city then of only 200,000 — were more familiar with both the domesticated and the wild flora than urban people tend to be today. They would have been able to visualize plants like saffron, poppy and aconitum from the mere mention of the narcotics or poisons made from them. For that reason, and because of their attractiveness for engravings, we have included them. On the other hand, we omitted some familiar crop plants with insignificant flowers, and we drew the line between flowering shrubs and trees, omitting the latter.

Not surprisingly, there are a few flowers like violet and daisy to which Shakespeare refers dozens of times; in those cases we merely cite attractive representative examples. At the same time, several of Shakespeare's best-known passages refer to groups or clusters of flowers; sometimes in a brief poetic description like Oberon's in *A Midsummer Night's Dream* (page 22);

sometimes in a song like that near the end of *Love's Labour's Lost* (page 32) or the one at the beginning of *The Two Noble Kinsmen* (pages 92, 94); and sometimes as the subject of a dialogue with action, at the centre of which is a 'flower-maiden', as in the case of Ophelia in her mad scene in *Hamlet* (page 42), Marina in *Pericles* (page 18), and Perdita in her long dialogue with Polixenes in *The Winter's Tale* (pages 56–72). The accompanying engravings show groups of flowers, some of which are presented and discussed individually elsewhere. Usually the flowers are mentioned in a human context, as one would expect in drama and in such ritual as a marriage song. In Shakespeare's time much more than today, many flowers, for instance violets, rosemary and rue, had symbolic associations, as is clear, for example, in the Ophelia episode. The commentary in this book examines such meanings. It also explicates what plant Shakespeare actually meant when he used a certain name; for instance, honeysuckle is synonymous with woodbine.

Our own study of the subject has greatly benefited from that of the Rev. Henry N. Ellacombe, *The Plant-Lore and Garden-Craft of Shakespeare* (second edition, 1884), a work that is remarkably comprehensive and reliable. Commentaries in some modern scholarly editions of Shakespeare, especially those in the Arden series, proved helpful with identification and meanings. For current botanical names and precise descriptions we have turned to such guides as *Flora of the British Isles* by A.R. Clapham, T.G. Tutin, and E.F. Warburg (1952), and the *Collins Pocket Guide to Wildflowers* by David McClintock and R.S.R. Fitter (fifth impression, 1965). Most line references to Shakespeare passages cited are to the *Riverside Shakespeare* (textual editor, G.B. Evans, 1974), but spelling follows Oxford standard and some textual readings reflect our own critical preference.

— F. David Hoeniger

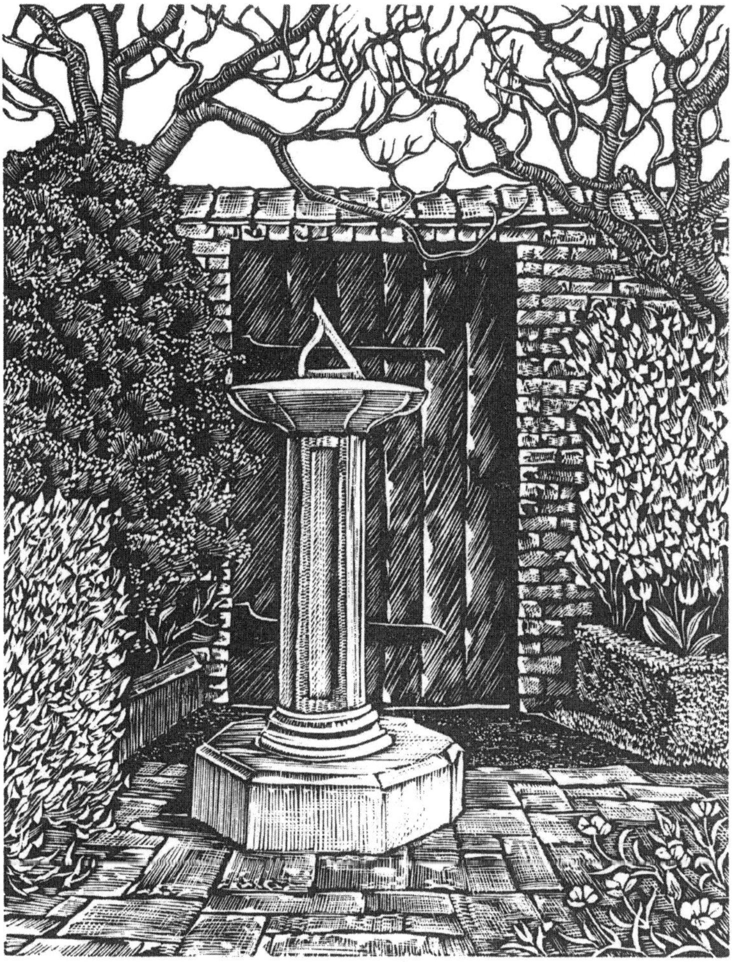

Sundial at Hall's Croft Garden.

## **Opium Poppy** (*Papaver somniferum*)

Aware of the effect of his poisonous insinuations of jealousy on Othello's mind, Iago comments to himself:

> Not poppy, nor mandragora,
> Nor all the drowsy syrups of the world
> Shall ever medicine thee to that sweet sleep
> Which thou ow'dst yesterday.
>
> *Othello*, 3. 3. 330–333

As this sole Shakespearean reference to the poppy shows, he had the narcotic in mind, and therefore neither the common corn poppy (*Papaver rhoeas*) of southern, nor the long-headed poppy (*Papaver dubium*) of northern England. Both have scarlet flowers, while those of the opium poppy are usually white- or lilac-coloured. However, in Shakespeare's time the plant merely served as a garden ornament, for then, as still a hundred years ago, opium was imported to England from the Far East. (For *mandragora*, see page 52.)

---

*ow'dst*: owned

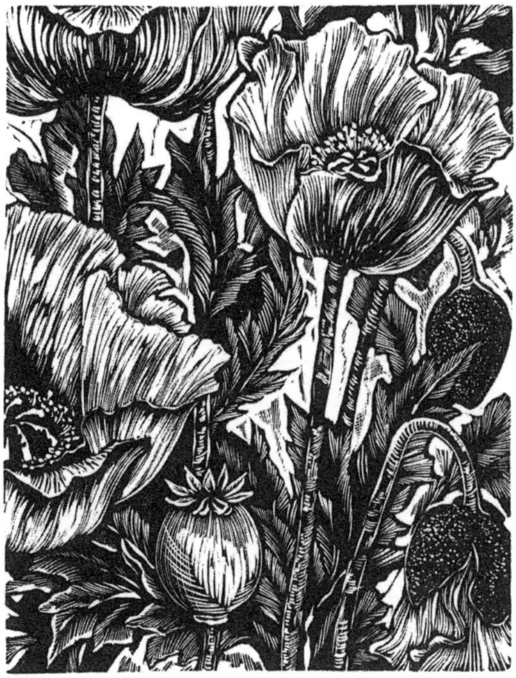

**Honeysuckle** or **Woodbine** (*Lonicera periclymenum*)

This is the sweet honeysuckle of woods and hedges with fragrant rosy-white flowers and pretty, fleshy, orange-red fruit. Climbing around branches and through shrubs, it puts out its sweet-scented flowers throughout the summer. Its use in the arbours or 'covertures', pictured here, of formal Elizabethan gardens is echoed in the scene in *Much Ado About Nothing* where Hero, Margaret and Ursula plot to lure Beatrice into believing that Benedick has fallen hopelessly in love with her. So that Beatrice will overhear Hero's and Ursula's feigned conversation, Margaret is asked to

> ... Bid her steal into the pleached bower,
> Where honeysuckles, ripened by the sun,
> forbid the sun to enter.
>
> 3. 1. 7–9

When she succeeds, Ursula, comparing their situation with an angler's delight in snaring a fish to 'devour a treacherous bait', whispers to Hero

> So angle we for Beatrice, who even now
> Is couched in the woodbine coverture.
>
> 3. 1. 26–30

Woodbine and honeysuckle usually were names for the same flower in Shakespeare's time, though 'woodbine' could also be applied to other climbing plants. This may explain why Shakespeare has Titania saying while embracing Bottom

> So doth the woodbine the sweet honeysuckle
> Gently entwist
>
> *A Midsummer Night's Dream*, 4. 1. 41–42

Because the honeysuckle clings so tightly to any tree or bush nearby, it became an emblem of loyal affection. Yet when in *King Henry IV, Second Part*, Mistress Quickly responds to Falstaff's rude suggestion that she has been thrown into the 'channel' or gutter with

> Ah, thou honeysuckle villain!
>
> 2. 1. 50–51

she comically mistakes the word for 'homicidal', though perhaps with the extra intimation of how much Falstaff, when he clung to her, had abused her.

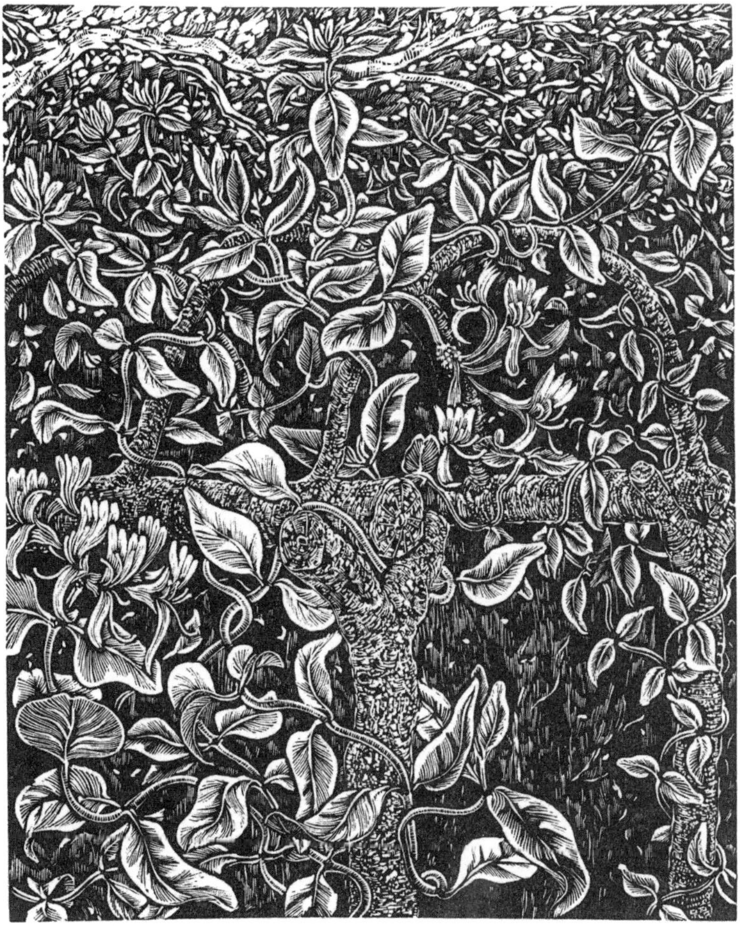

## **Pot** or **Garden Marigold** (*Calendula officinalis*)

And winking Mary-buds begin to ope
their golden eyes.

Song in *Cymbeline*, 2. 3. 23

Shakespeare's six references are not to the familiar marsh marigold, but to a plant popular in gardens of country cottages and farmhouses in Shakespeare's time. It was also called 'gold', as in Chaucer and Spenser.

The flower's quality of opening and shutting at the sun's bidding made it a favourite with religious writers of the later Renaissance. They often interpreted it as an emblem of constancy, but it could also signify sycophantic fawning, as hinted at in Sonnet 25, 5–6:

Great princes' favourites their fair leaves spread
But as the marigold at the sun's eye.

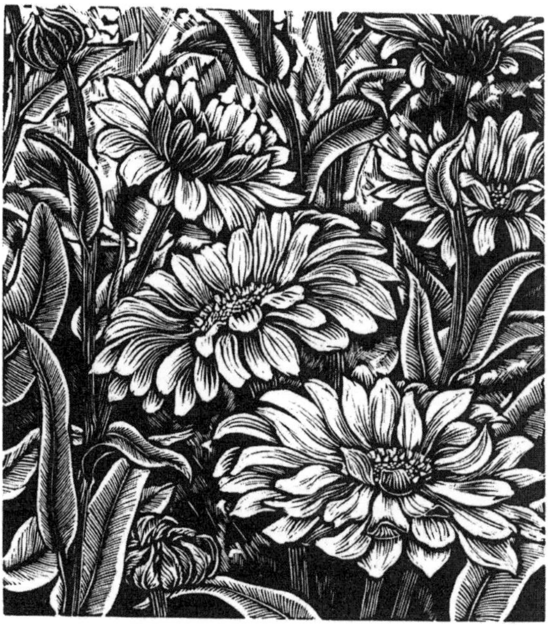

## **Violet** (*Viola odorata*)

Laertes: A violet in the youth of primy nature,
Forward, not permanent, sweet, not lasting,
The perfume and suppliance of a minute —
No more.

*Hamlet*, 1. 3. 7–10

Orsino: That strain again! It had a dying fall;
O, it came o'er my ear like the sweet sound
That breathes upon a bank of violets,
Stealing and giving odour.

*Twelfth Night*, 1. 1. 4–7

Some of Shakespeare's many references to violets clearly indicate the sweet violet (*Viola odorata*), since it is the only fragrant one in Britain. It is usually purple, but white and double forms have been developed under cultivation. Bacon wrote of it in his essay 'Of Gardens': 'that which above all others yields the sweetest smell in the air is the violet, specially the white double violet, which comes twice a year; about the middle of April, and about Bartholomew-tide [i.e., late August].' Other references in Shakespeare may well be to the common dog violet (*Viola riviniana*), but they are too general for precise identification.

An early flower of the spring, it was commonly associated with death and especially with short-livedness, as in Laertes's warning lines to Ophelia about Hamlet's love. Later, over her grave, he exclaims:

And from her fair and unpolluted flesh
May violets spring!

*Hamlet*, 5. 1. 239–240

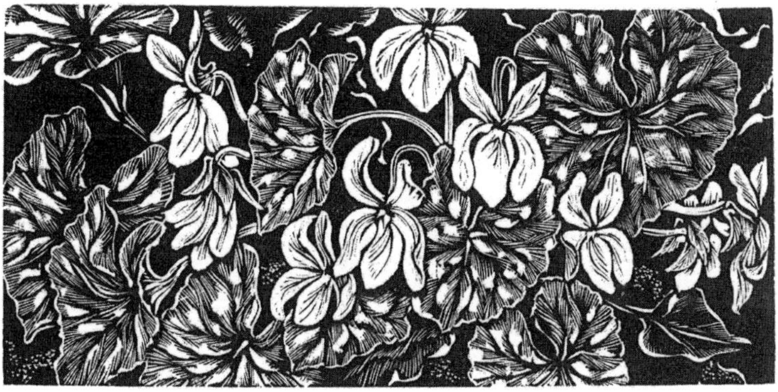

**Flowers for a Grave:**
**Marigold** and **Violet** (*Calendula officinalis* and *Viola odorata*)

Mourning her nurse, Lychorida, Marina in *Pericles* enters with a basket of flowers:

> No; I will rob Tellus of her weed
> To strow thy green with flowers. The yellows, blues,
> The purple violets, and marigolds,
> Shall as a carpet hang upon thy grave
> While summer days doth last.

4. 1. 13–17

---

*Tellus*: the earth; *weed*: dress of flowers; *green*: i.e., of the grave

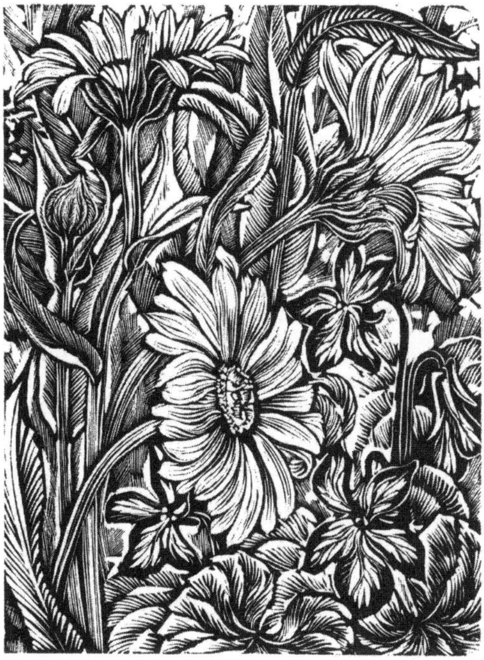

**Love-in-idleness** *(Viola tricolor)*

Known also as heartsease or wild pansy, love-in-idleness is a common favourite in England. It blooms from May to September, its flowers varying from white and yellow to purple. Pansy symbolizes remembrance — see Ophelia's lines on page 98 — but love-in-idleness signifies rather unsatisfied love or desire. In *The Taming of the Shrew*, for instance, Lucentio confides to his servant, Tranio, how, in his sudden overwhelming passion for Bianca, he

> Found the effect of love in idleness
>
> 1. 1. 150–155

More famous are Oberon's lines in *A Midsummer Night's Dream* in which he describes how he watched the flight of Cupid's arrow intended for a vestal virgin:

> Yet marked I where the bolt of Cupid fell:
> It fell upon a little western flower,
> Before milk-white, now purple with love's wound,
> And maidens call it love-in-idleness.
>
> 2. 1. 165–168

Oberon commands Puck to fetch this flower. For the ensuing action, see page 22. Both story and allusion to the pansy's changed colours are prettily fanciful.

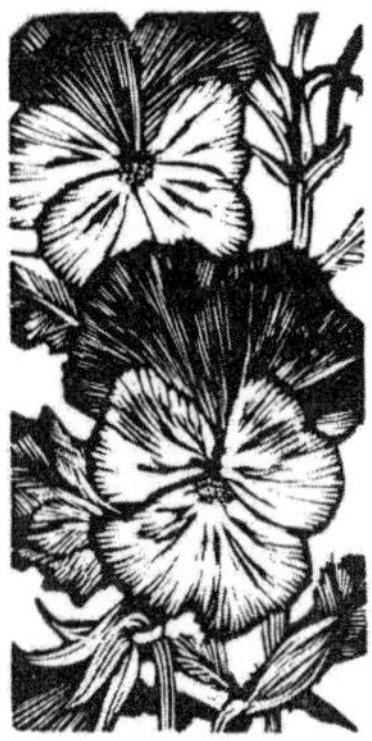

**Titania's Bank of Flowers**

Oberon: I know a bank where the wild thyme blows,
Where oxlip and the nodding violet grows,
Quite over-canopied with luscious woodbine,
With sweet musk-roses and with eglantine.
There sleeps Titania sometime of the night,
Lull'd in these flowers with dances and delight.

*A Midsummer Night's Dream*, 2. 1. 249–254

Puck has just brought Oberon the flower called love-in-idleness as shown on the previous page, with the juice of which he intends to 'streak' the Fairy Queen Titania's eyes 'and make her full of hateful fantasies'. As a result she will, upon awaking, dote upon Bottom who has been transformed into an ass. The flower passage suits Oberon as King of Fairies and May King.

The picture on the facing page shows large, white musk-roses, so named for their fragrance, in the centre, and an eglantine or sweet-briar with double-toothed leaves to their right. The small plants close to the ground with creeping runners are lilac-flowered wild thyme. True oxlips are seen below the roses and to the right; sweet violets 'nodding' to their left. All these are 'over-canopied' with woodbine or honeysuckle as shown top left and right.

---

Additional engravings, Shakespearean references and descriptions appear as follows: woodbine, pages 12, 13; wild thyme, pages 50, 51; oxlip, pages 68, 69, 94, 95; musk-rose, pages 80, 81; and eglantine, pages 86, 87.

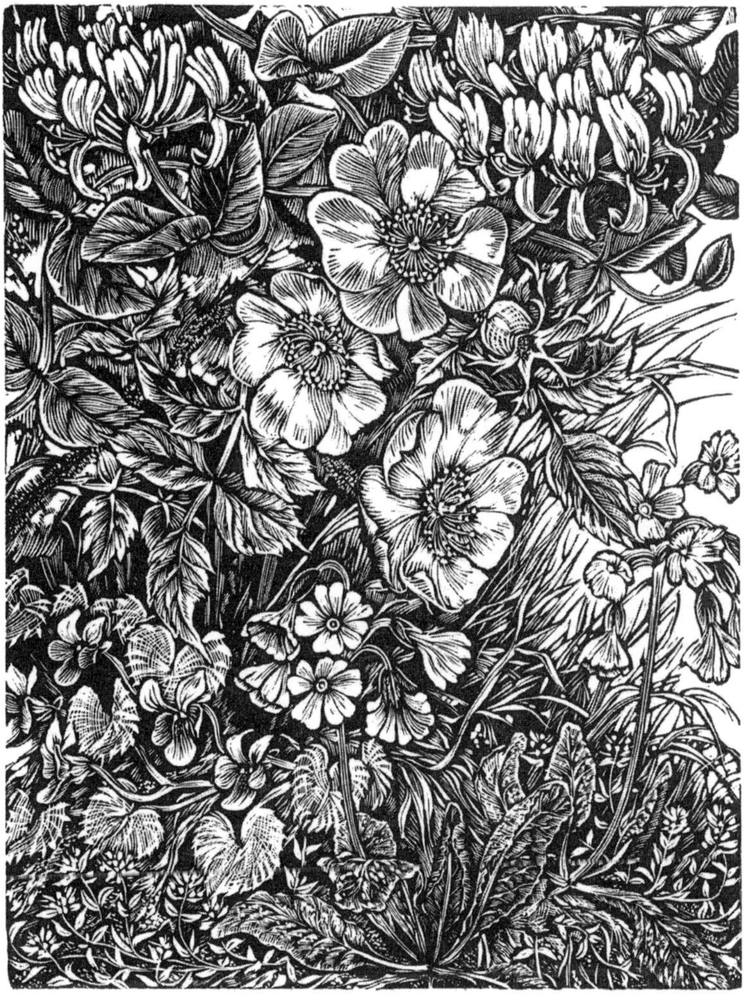

This imagined spot shows flowers that would not all bloom simultaneously — as befits the realm of Oberon, where anything is possible.

**Cowslip** (*Primula veris*)

Botanically a primrose, as its scientific name indicates, the cowslip was in Shakespeare's time as it is today a favourite wild as well as garden plant because of its fragrance and its beautiful deep yellow flowers, orange at the base, with reddish or golden spots.

Shakespeare alludes to both the scent and the colour of the cowslip in a passage from *A Midsummer Night's Dream* and to its spots in the lines that form part of Iachimo's deceitful description of Imogen to Posthumus in *Cymbeline*:

On her left breast
A mole cinque-spotted, like the crimson drops
I' th' bottom of a cowslip.

2. 2. 37–39

Here Iachimo tricks Posthumus into believing that his beloved has been sexually disloyal. But he actually managed to see her breast only when, secretly and at night, he climbed out of a trunk which he had persuaded her to store in her bedroom.

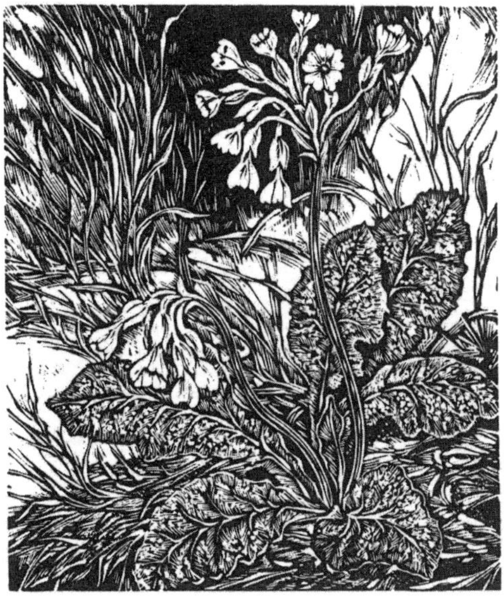

**Cowslip** (*Primula veris*)

In the scene which introduces the fairy world for the first time in *A Midsummer Night's Dream*, a fairy describes her tasks poetically to Puck and to us:

> And I serve the Fairy Queen,
> To dew her orbs upon the green.
> The cowslips tall her pensioners be,
> In their gold coats spots you see:
> Those be rubies, fairy favours,
> In those freckles live their savours.
> I must go seek some dewdrops here,
> And hang a pearl in every cowslip's ear.
>
> 2.1.8–15

The 'pensioners' are the fairy counterparts to Queen Elizabeth's royal bodyguards whose uniforms were adorned with gold lace and jewels. In Shakespeare's time, the poet Drayton too wrote of the cowslip as the special flower of fairies.

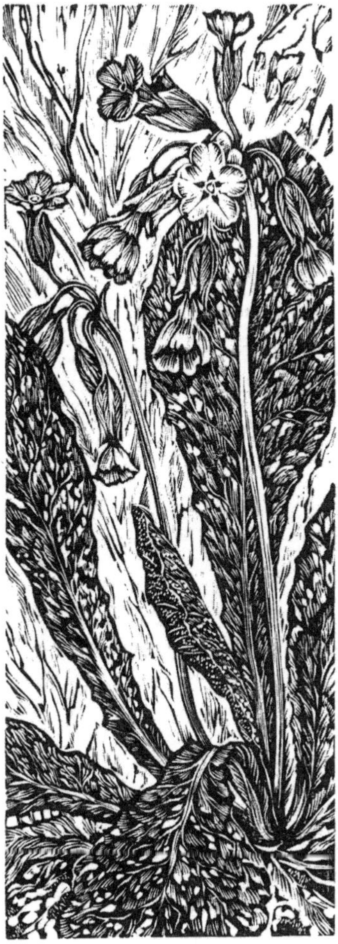

**Violets, Cowslips, Primroses** (*Viola* sp., *Primula veris, Primula vulgaris*)

In an early scene in *Cymbeline*, the evil queen who dabbles in poisons orders her ladies to gather the flowers she has listed on a sheet of paper. And when they return, she tells them:

> The violets, cowslips, and the primroses
> Bear to my closet.
>
> 1. 5. 83–84

Because of its paleness, the primrose was sometimes balefully associated with death, but if there were sinister associations with the two other flowers, we do not know them. Here the three flowers are shown in an interior with a beautiful, rotund Bellarmine drinking-jug.

---

For separate pictures and texts of the three flowers, see pages 16, 17; 24, 25, 26, 27; and 48, 49.

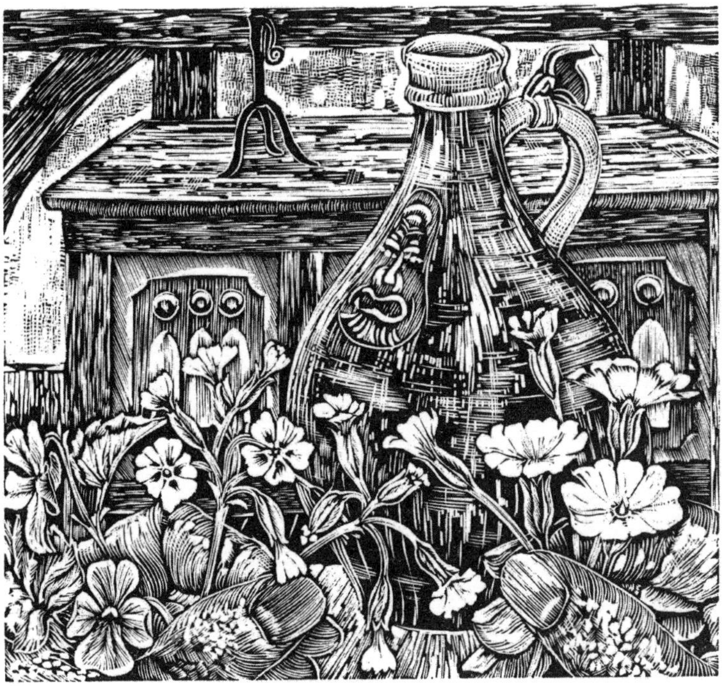

**Common Pink** (*Dianthus plumarius*)

When, during his nimble wit-combat with Romeo, Mercutio refers mockingly to himself as

> the very pink of courtesy

and Romeo rebuts:

> Pink for flower
>
> *Romeo and Juliet*, 2. 4. 57–58

meaning that Mercutio is the very flower, the acme or perfection of courtesy, there is no need to know what kind of pink Shakespeare may have had in mind.

The word 'pink' is applied to several species of the genus *Dianthus*, and, as the *Oxford English Dictionary* tells us, in Shakespeare's time the term was also given to other plants allied to or resembling the pink. It suffices that among familiar garden plants of the genus, Shakespeare probably knew the common pink here pictured.

It is a plant of numerous varieties, with pure white, pink, crimson, or variegated, sweet-smelling flowers. While not all pinks are pink in colour, yet, as in the case of 'violet', the colour's name was derived from the flower. The flower may have been so named from the delicately cut or 'peaked' edges of its petals.

---

For the cultivated variety of clove-pink or clove-scented pink, see pages 60, 61.

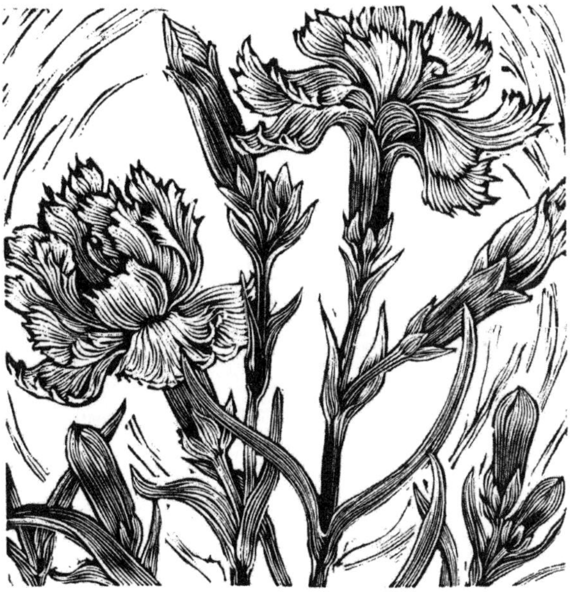

**The Cuckoo's Song of Spring:**
**Daisies** and **Violets** (*Bellis perennis* and *Viola* sp.)

Close to the end of *Love's Labour's Lost,* the subplot characters form two groups. The first group recites the song of spring, the second one the song of winter. Part of the song of spring reads:

When daisies pied, and violets blue,
And lady-smocks all silver-white,
And cuckoo-buds of yellow hue
Do paint the meadows with delight,
The cuckoo then on every tree
Mocks married men....

5.2.894–899

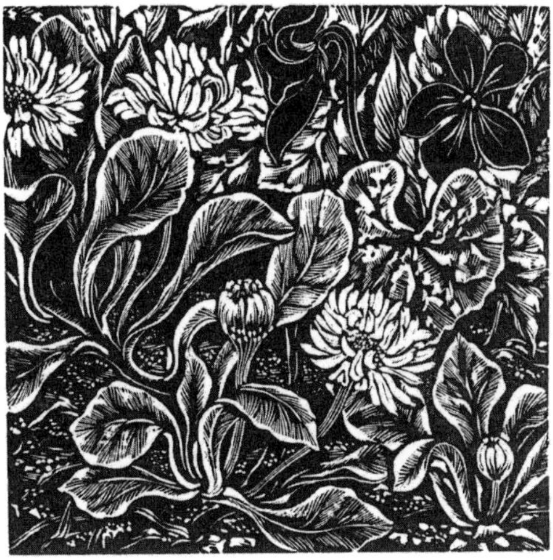

**Buttercups** and **Lady-smocks**
(*Ranunculus acris* and *Cardamine pratensis*)

Lady-smocks or meadow cresses grow in wet meadows. Their flowers vary from deep lilac to white. They were also called cuckoo-flowers (as in *King Lear*, 4. 4. 4) because they bloom in April when the cuckoo returns to Britain. By cuckoo-buds, on the other hand, Shakespeare probably meant buttercups.

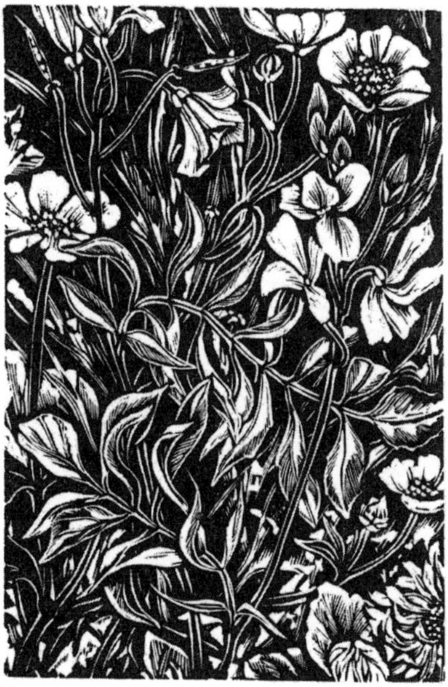

## **Holy** or **Blessed Thistle**

(formerly *Carduus benedictus*, now *Cnicus benedictus*)

Not one of the many species of wild-growing thistles, but a plant from southern Europe that was introduced early in English herb-gardens as a heal-all, *Carduus* had the reputation of being able to cure even the plague. In *Much Ado about Nothing*, Hero and Margaret are mocking Beatrice when to her own surprise she has become lovesick for Benedick:

> Beatrice: ... By my troth, I am sick.
> Margaret: Get you some of this distill'd *Carduus benedictus*,
> and lay it to your heart; it is the only thing for a qualm.
> Hero: There thou prick'st her with a thistle.
> Beatrice: *Benedictus!* why *benedictus?* You have some moral in
> this *benedictus*.
> Margaret: Moral? no, by my troth I have no moral meaning.
> I meant plain holy-thistle....
>
> 3.4.72–80

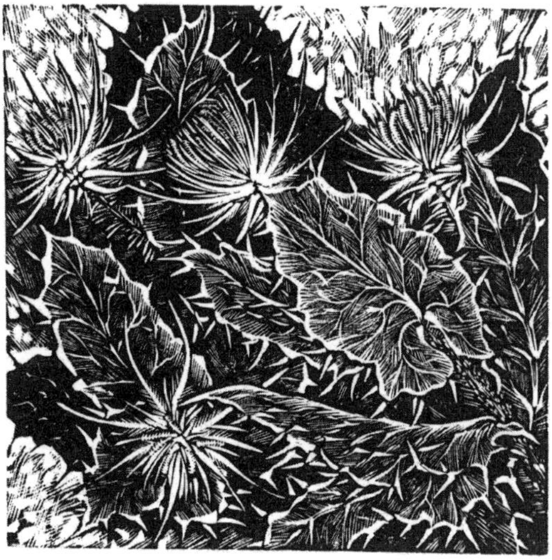

**Snake's-head Fritillary** or **Checker-board Flower**
(*Fritillaria meleagris*)

The following lines occur close to the end of Shakespeare's narrative poem *Venus and Adonis*, after Adonis has been killed by a boar:

> By this the boy that by her side lay killed
> Was melted like a vapour from her sight,
> And in his blood that on the ground lay spilled
> A purple flower sprung up, checkered with white,
> Resembling well his pale cheeks and the blood
> Which in round drops upon their whiteness stood,
>
> 1165–1170

whereupon Venus breaks the flower off by the stalk and places it on her breast.

Shakespeare based these lines on those in Ovid's *Metamorphoses*, where an anemone (literally a 'wind-flower') springs from Adonis's blood; and so Shakespeare's 'purple flower' has usually been likewise glossed as an anemone. Neither poet's description fits the wood anemone, whose exterior is pink with white inside. But the spring-blooming checker-board flower of southern England fits Shakespeare's lines, with its drooping, purple and white blooms.

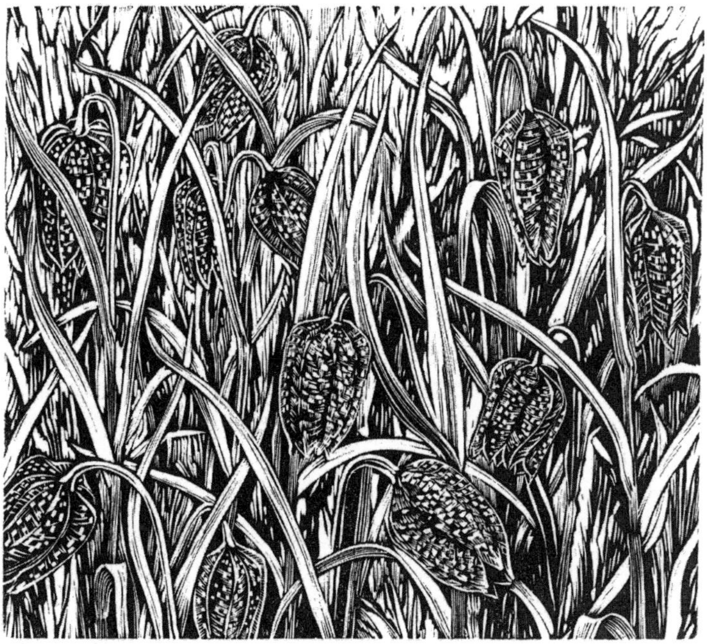

**Samphire — Rock Samphire** (*Crithmum maritimum*)

Pretending to stand close to the cliffs of Dover, Edgar describes the scene in persuasive detail to his blind and suicide-minded father, Gloucester:

> Half-way down
> Hangs one that gathers samphire, dreadful trade!
> Methinks he seems no bigger than his head.
>
> *King Lear,* 4. 6. 14–16

The leaves of this plant, which grows widely on cliffs and rocks by the sea, were used for a pleasant pickle. The trade of gathering samphire, hanging by a long rope, was indeed dangerous.

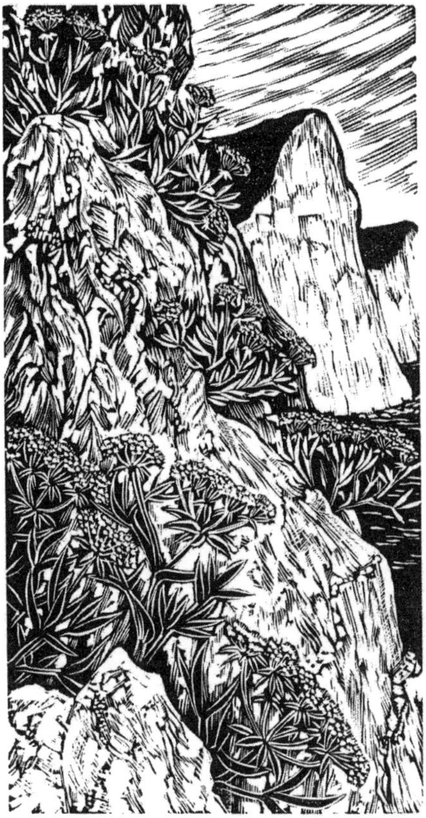

**Ophelia's Fantastic Garlands:**
**Purple Orchid** and **English Daisy** (*Orchis mascula* and *Bellis perennis*)

The following lines are part of Gertrude's moving speech in Act IV, Scene 7 of *Hamlet* where she describes how the mad Ophelia drowned:

> Therewith fantastic garlands did she make
> Of crow-flowers, nettles, daisies, and long purples,
> That liberal shepherds give a grosser name,
> But our cold maids do dead men's fingers call them.
>
> — Lines 143–146,
> Oxford text based on folio edition

When she tried to hang these garlands on boughs overhanging a stream, a branch broke and Ophelia and her 'weedy trophies' fell into the water.

This engraving shows daisies with long purples. Notwithstanding controversy among critical commentators, the reference to long purples is clear as long as one does not insist on Shakespeare being a meticulous botanist. The roots of the early purple orchid (*Orchis mascula*) do not fit the passage literally, but those of another common mauve orchid (*Orchis maculata*) in English woods do. 'Dead men's fingers' has been a popular way of referring to the palmate root of purple orchids whose lobes resemble spread fingers. The 'grosser' names, avoided by 'cold' chaste maids, are listed in Lyte's *Herbal* of 1578 as priest's pintle, dogstones and goat's cullions.

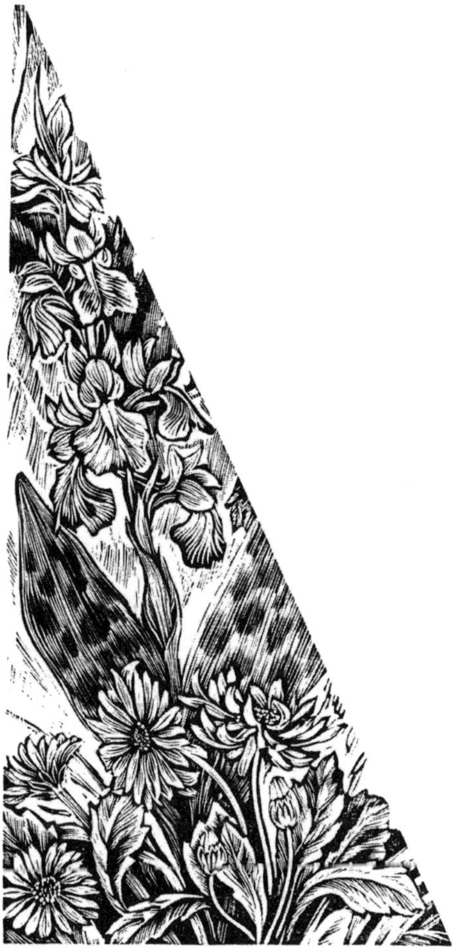

**Crow-flower** with **White Dead-Nettle**
(*Lychnis flos-cuculi* and *Lamium album*)

This engraving shows the crow-flowers with much divided petals of deep pink — now commonly known as 'ragged robins' — and dead nettles which do not sting and have white or purple flowers.

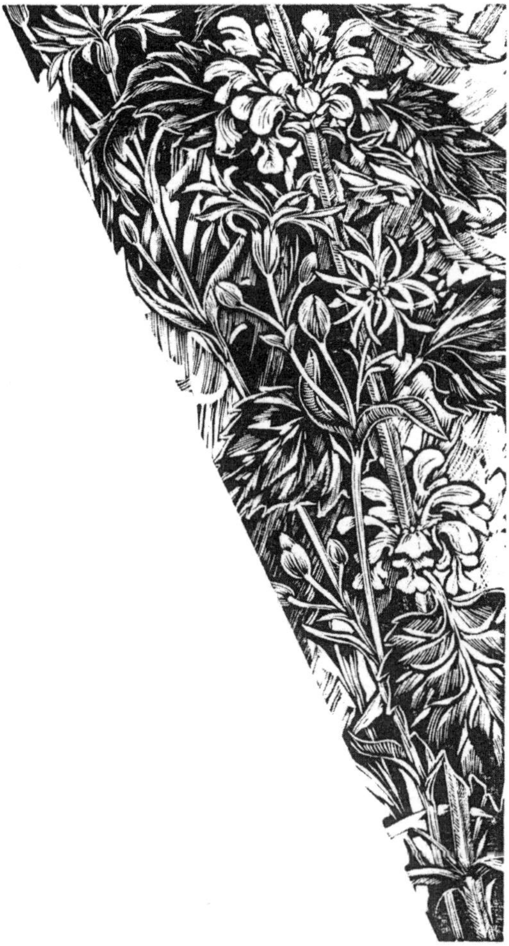

**Chamomile** (*Chamaemelum nobile* or *Anthemis nobilis*)

> … for though the chamomile, the more it is trodden on, the faster it grows, [yet] youth, the more it is wasted, the sooner it wears.
>
> Falstaff in *Henry IV, First Part*, 2. 4. 399–402

Much used on the edges of flower-beds in Elizabethan gardens, it is a running plant that spreads quickly. Thus the proverbial image that the more it is stepped upon the more it multiplies, which became especially popular among euphuistic writers, whose style Falstaff parodies. It has a fine aroma, and then as now was believed to have medical virtues. It was an emblem of humility, since being so lowly that it is trodden on, it rises best.

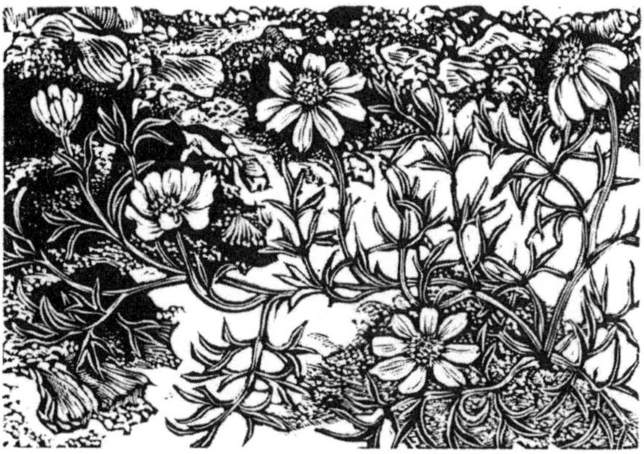

**Primrose** (*Primula vulgaris*)

A universal favourite, the primrose is a low perennial of solitary flowers, pale yellow with a deeper yellow eye. In England, it grows abundantly in woods as well as on sea-cliffs, and also makes a good garden plant from February to April.

Interestingly enough, Shakespeare seems to have invented the phrase 'the primrose path', placed in Ophelia's mouth when she tells Laertes not, like 'ungracious pastors', to show her

> ... the steep and thorny way to heaven,
> Whiles, [like] a puff'd and reckless libertine,
> Himself the primrose path of dalliance treads,
> And reaks not his own rede.
>
> *Hamlet*, 1. 3. 48–51

The idea behind the phrase, of which Shakespeare evidently became fond for he repeated it elsewhere, comes from the biblical 'wide is the gate and broad is the way that leadeth to destruction' (Matthew 7: 13–14) and the story of Hercules' choice between virtue and vice, where he has to decide whether to take the smooth and easy way that leads to wickedness or not. Compare the Porter's drunken remarks in *Macbeth*, that unconsciously allude to the evil events that have just occurred in the castle:

> I had thought to have let in some of all professions that
> go the primrose way to th' everlasting bonfire.
>
> 2. 3. 17–19

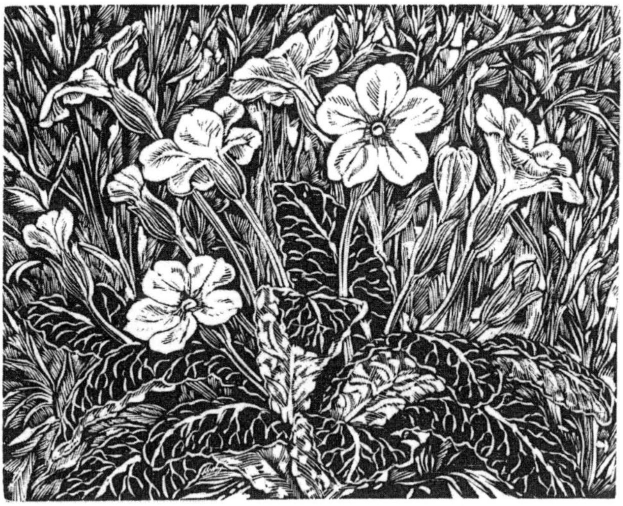

**Garden Thyme** under **Hyssop**
(*Thymus vulgaris* under *Hyssopus officinalis*)

An upright, evergreen shrub native to the western Mediterranean, this variety of thyme was cultivated widely for both its antiseptic and its culinary virtues. As

> sweet thyme true
>
> *Two Noble Kinsmen*, 1. 1. 6

it was also much favoured by bee-keepers, as were the various forms of its wild cousin, *Thymus serpyllum*.

Thyme was traditionally associated with the benefits the virtuous can derive from adversity (Plutarch, *Moralia*, 6. 180–183) and Elizabethan gardeners grew hyssop — regarded as a cleansing plant since ancient times and therefore symbolizing spiritual purification — together with thyme as mutual aids in growth (Lyly, *Euphues*). This is alluded to by Iago when, while humouring Othello's feeble and disconsolate rival, Roderigo, he devises the following comparison:

> Our bodies are our gardens, to which our wills are gardeners so that if we will plant nettles or sow lettuce, set hyssop and weed up thyme, supply it with one gender of herbs or distract it with many, either to have it sterile with idleness or manured with industry — why, the power and corrigible authority of this lies in our wills [as it does in curbing our lusts].
>
> *Othello*, 1. 3. 317–322

Weeding up thyme, Iago says, would be as contrary to the garden's welfare as planting nettles.

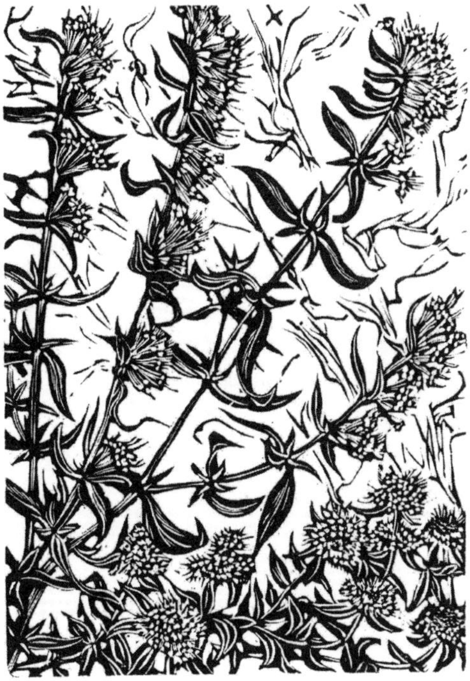

## **Mandrake** (*Mandragora officinarum*)

Shakespeare's references to 'mandrake' are to the plant or its root, those to 'mandragora' to the syrup made from the root-derived juice that was drunk as a sleeping potion — see the lines from *Othello* cited on page 10 under 'Poppy' — and used as an anaesthetic in surgery.

A native of Mediterranean countries, its root was known in England from the early Middle Ages on though the plant itself was introduced into herb gardens only in the sixteenth century. Because its whiskery, forked root was thought to bear a resemblance to the lower half of the human body, it was highly valued as a love potion and associated with fertility and sexual prowess. To this Shakespeare alludes in Falstaff's scathing remarks on Shallow's bragging about his exploits as a young man:

> ... yet lecherous as a monkey, and the whores called him
> mandrake ...
>
> *Henry IV, Second Part*, 3. 2. 314–315

But the notion of an assimilation of 'man' and 'drake' (or 'dragon') is suspect.

The demand for mandrake roots led to the skilful culture of white bryony to make counterfeit roots that looked much more like miniature humans, both male and female, selling for high prices.

The following quotation from *Romeo and Juliet* reflects the widespread superstition that anyone who plucked the root would hear a deafening scream and die soon after. Hallucinating in her state of extreme fright, as she faces the Friar's 'poisonous' draught, Juliet imagines

> ... shrieks like mandrakes' torn out of the earth,
> That living mortals, hearing them, run mad.
>
> 4. 3. 47–48

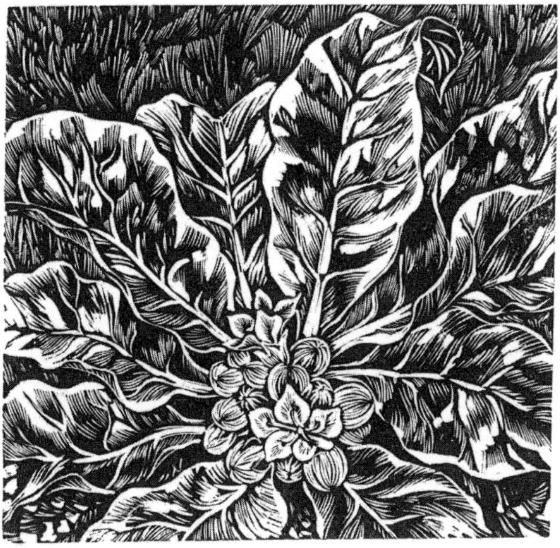

**Yellow Flag** (*Iris pseudacorus*)

In *Antony and Cleopatra*, Octavius Caesar uses the following image when he comments contemptuously on how the common people waver in their response towards political leaders who rise to power, like himself, and those who decline, like Antony:

> This common body,
> Like to a vagabond flag upon the stream,
> Goes to and back, lackeying the varying tide,
> To rot itself with motion.
>
> 1. 4. 44-47

As Ellacombe pointed out, in the Bible 'flag' is a general term for reeds and similar plants, and the word was sometimes used in this wide sense in Shakespeare's time. But here it is very probable that the yellow flag or iris is meant which, as the engraving shows, grows close to Clopton Bridge (built in the sixteenth century by Sir Hugh Clopton) in Stratford-upon-Avon, and which locals know by this name.

---

*body*: people; *lackeying*: following like a lackey

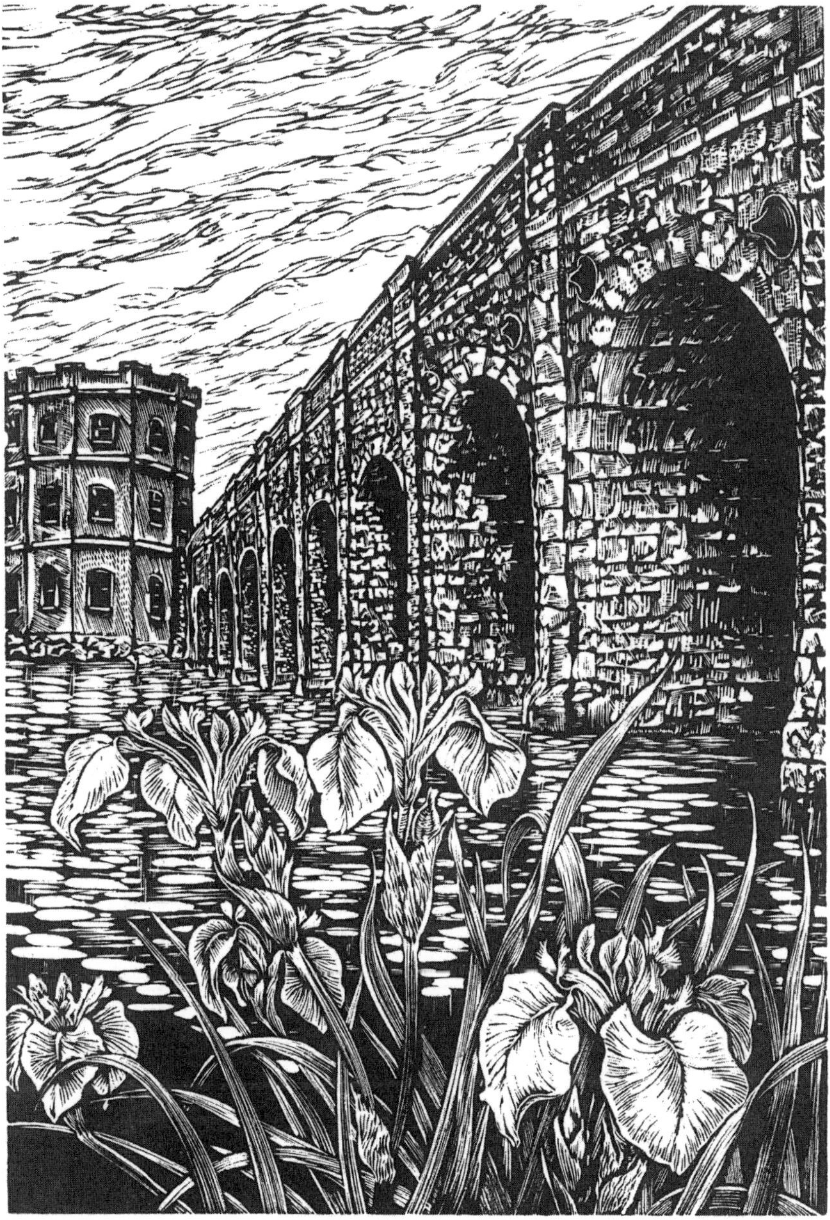

**Perdita's Welcoming Speech:**
**Rosemary** and **Rue** (*Rosmarinus officinalis* and *Ruta graveolens*)

The episode in the pastoral scene of *The Winter's Tale*, where Perdita — during a sheep-shearing festival — bestows flowers on the various guests (4. 4. 73–128), forms the longest flower passage in Shakespeare. Sheep-shearing takes place in late spring but, typical of the pastoral convention with its idealization, Shakespeare in this scene combines allusions to spring with others to the harvest season.

Perdita selects the flowers from her garden in such a way as to suit as well as she can the different age groups of her guests. She turns first to the oldest, Polixenes, the disguised King of Bohemia, and his friend the Lord Camillo, greeting them with rosemary and rue, flowers that symbolize grace and remembrance:

> Give me those flowers there, Dorcas. Reverend Sirs,
> For you there's rosemary and rue; these keep
> Seeming and savour all the winter long:
> Grace and remembrance be to you both,
> And welcome to our shearing!
>
> 4. 4. 73–77

Highly favoured in Shakespeare's time for its lasting aromatic scent and its evergreen leaves, rosemary was used to decorate dishes served for Christmas banquets, as alluded to by the bawd in *Pericles* when he says to the chaste Marina:

> Marry, come up, my dish of chastity with rosemary and bays!
>
> 4. 6. 150–151

But it was chiefly associated with age, death and remembrance.

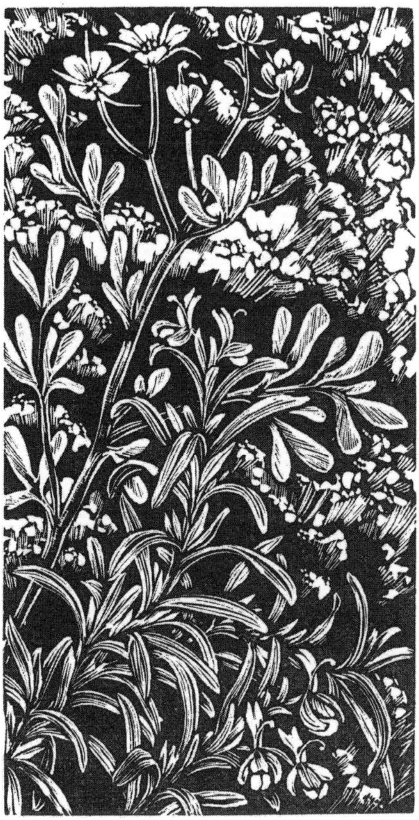

## **Carnations** and **Streaked Gillyvors** (*Dianthus* sp.)

Next, and replying to Polixenes' courteous acknowledgement, Perdita explains why her garden lacks flowers of autumn, a season that would seem more fitting:

> Sir, the year growing ancient,
> Nor yet on summer's death nor on the birth
> Of trembling winter, the fairest flowers o' th' season
> Are our carnations and streak'd gillyvors,
> Which some call nature's bastards: of that kind
> Our rustic garden's barren; and I care not
> To get slips of them.

Perdita's rejection of carnations and gillyflowers starts off her famous debate with Polixenes on art and nature. She rejects them because they are products not of nature but of 'artificial' cross-breeding. In her view, such human intervention can only breed bastards. Polixenes asks her to correct this notion, using the eloquent argument that the powers of humankind to improve nature have likewise been created by nature. Unaware of her own royal origin, Perdita persists in her refusal, but the play ends with a revelation, assisted by art, of true identities.

There was great interest in grafting and hybridization in Elizabethan times. Relevant to our context, moreover, may be that the gillyflower had the reputation of being the flower above all others that showed variety, and that it was 'thought to produce cross-breeds without human aid'.

---

J. H. P. Pafford, in the new Arden edition of *A Winter's Tale*, page 170, cites from Shakespeare's contemporary, Francis Bacon, 'take gilly-flower seed of one kinde of gilly-flower ... and sow it; and there will come up gilly-flowers, some of one colour, and some of another ... as purple, carnation of several stripes', and concludes: 'in other words, they are nature's bastards.'

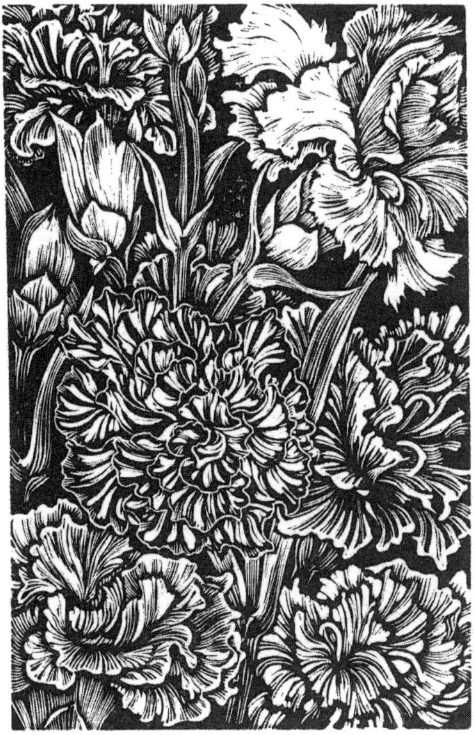

**Wall-gillyflower** (*Cheiranthus cheiri*)

Carnations were so called because of their rose-pink colour reminiscent of flesh tones. Yet the etymology is uncertain. Some think that the name was derived from 'coronation', since carnations had a high place in garlands in ancient Greece and Rome. Others think that the name was derived aphetically from 'incarnation'. The English garden carnation was developed from the wild carnation which is native to the Mediterranean, though it was naturalized at some English castles in the Middle Ages.

The botanical interpretation of the lines (page 58) is, however, uncertain for two reasons: in spite of Shakespeare's 'and', most scholars have taken 'gillyvors' as a synonym of 'carnations', the familiar cultivated form of the clove-pink (*Dianthus caryophyllus*). Gillyflowers came to their name from their scent of cloves (*girofle* in French). Yet in Shakespeare's time the name was applied loosely to other clove-scented flowers as well, including the wallflower (or wall-gillyflower) and the white stock (or stock-gillyflower). Therefore Shakespeare may have had two different plants in mind.

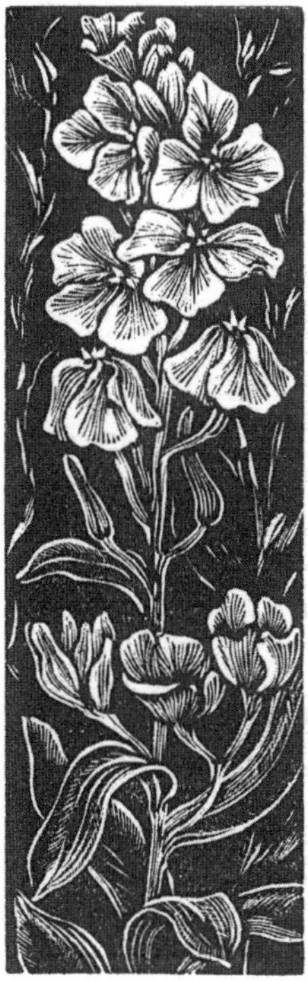

**Lavender** (*Lavandula angustifolia* or *spica*)

Ending her debate with Polixenes, Perdita turns to the middle-aged among her guests and bestows upon them flowers of summer.

> Here's flowers for you;
> Hot lavender, mints, savory, marjoram,
> The marigold that goes to bed wi' th' sun
> And with him rises weeping: these are flowers
> Of middle summer, and I think they are given
> To men of middle age. Y'are very welcome.

Lavender, as shown here, is a familiar small shrub with small pale-bluish flowers and narrow oblong leaves. It is cultivated mainly for its perfume, and dried leaves continue to give off their scent for years, but is also associated with cleanliness, its name being allied to the French verb, *laver*, — to wash. (For an explanation of 'hot', see page 64.)

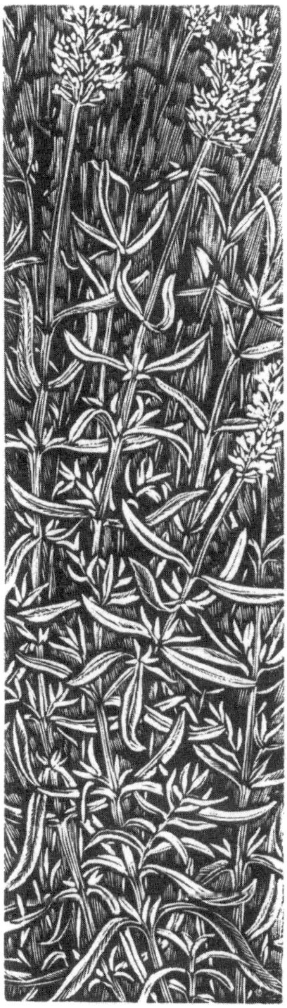

## Mary Arden's Kitchen

In the early herbals, descriptions of plants included their 'temperatures' or relative degrees of warmth and moisture that dictated their different pharmacological uses. Lavender was described as 'hot and dry in the second degree'. Mints, savory and marjoram are shown here with marigolds and the tools for chopping herbs in the kitchen of the house where Mary Arden, Shakespeare's mother, lived.

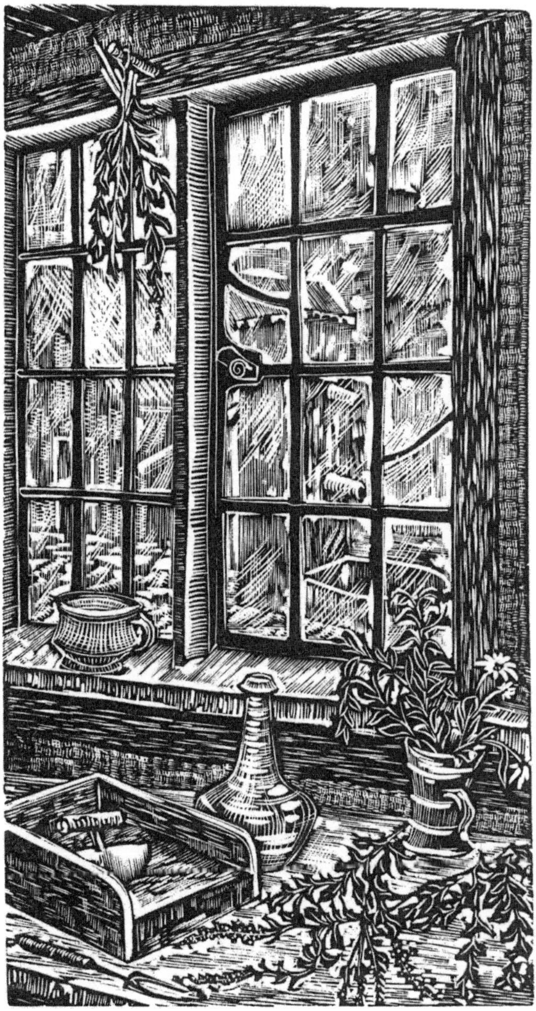

**Wild** or **'Tenby' Daffodil** (*Narcissus pseudonarcissus*)

Finally, Perdita addresses the younger members, including her lover, Florizel, telling them how much she regrets that she lacks early spring flowers befitting them:

> I would I had some flowers o' th' spring, that might
> Become your time of day....
> ... O Proserpina
> For the flowers now that, frighted, thou let'st fall
> From Dis's wagon! Daffodils,
> That come before the swallow dares, and take
> The winds of March with beauty; violets, dim
> But sweeter than the lids of Juno's eyes
> Or Cytherea's breath; pale primroses,
> That die unmarried, ere they can behold
> Bright Phoebus in his strength (a malady
> Most incident to maids);

Perdita's speech is thick with allusions to pagan mythology. She evokes Proserpina, daughter of Ceres, the goddess of vegetation, who, while gathering flowers, was seized by Pluto (or Dis) and carried into the underworld. Juno, queen of the gods, was renowned for her beauty, as was Cytherea, the surname of Venus or Aphrodite. Phoebus was the name of the sun-god.

The wild daffodil is smaller than most garden varieties that were introduced into Elizabethan gardens from the continent. Its name derives from Middle English 'affodyle', which means 'that which comes early'. Several English poets have celebrated it, among them Herrick, Wordsworth, Shelley and Keats.

---

For primroses, see page 48; for violets, page 16.

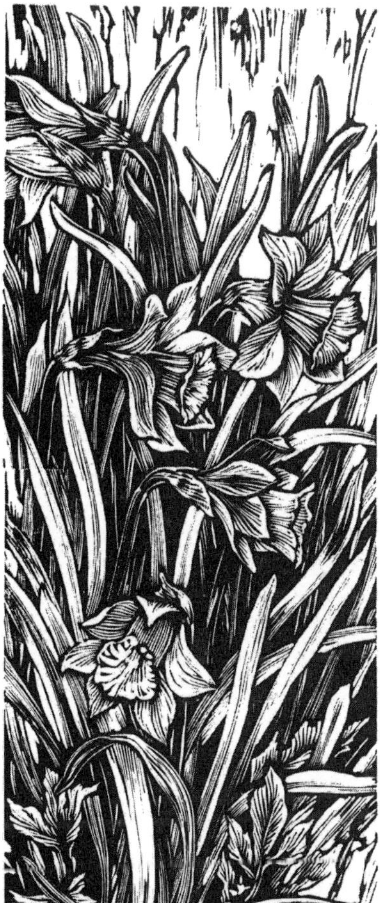

**Oxlips** (*Primula elatior*)

Shakespeare may be referring to either the true oxlip or to the false one or 'mulleyn', a hybrid between cowslip (*Primula veris*) and primrose (*Primula vulgaris*). Both have yellow flowers and are similar in other ways. The latter is more common, the true oxlip being found mainly in England's eastern counties.

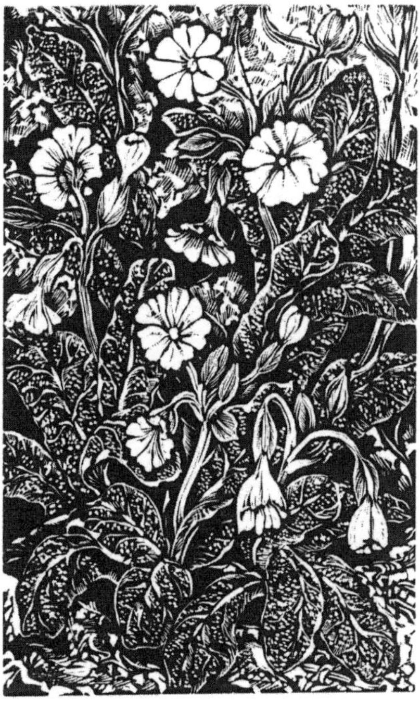

**Crown Imperials** (*Fritillaria imperialis*)

The crown imperial is a stately flower, bred in varieties of red and yellow, that is often given the pride of place in gardens. It was introduced early to England from the Near East. In *The Winter's Tale*, Perdita includes it in her catalogue of spring flowers which continues:

> ... bold oxlips, and
> the crown imperial;

George Chapman, Shakespeare's contemporary, called it 'fair crown imperial, emperor of flowers' in *Ovid's Banquet of Sense*.

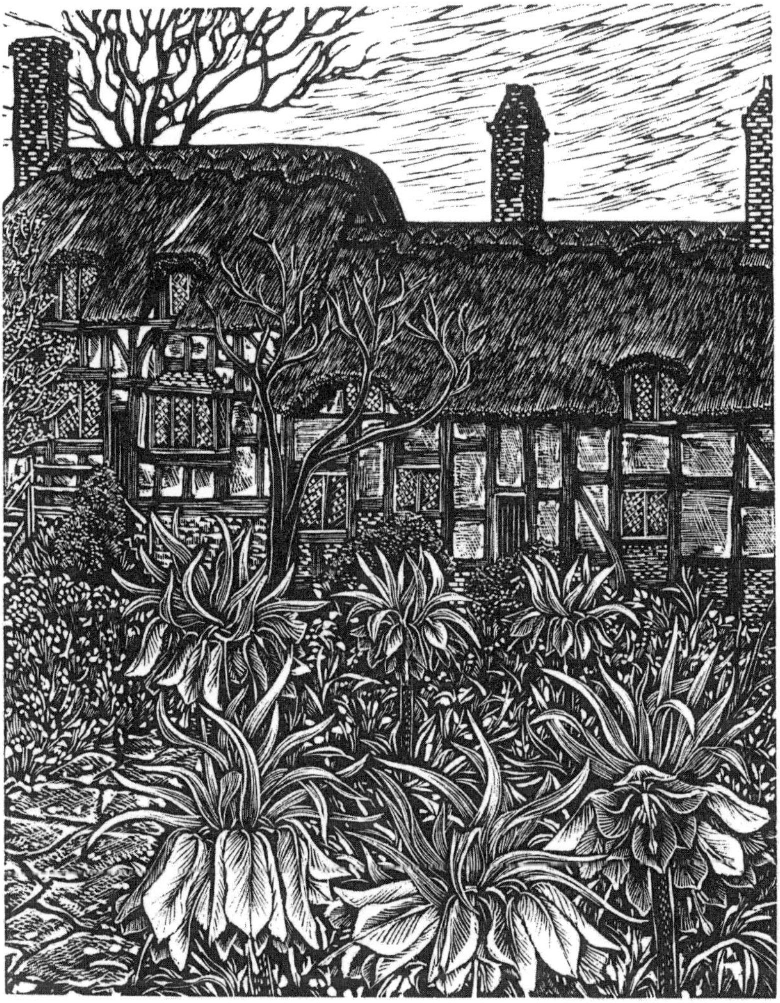

Crown Imperials in the garden of Anne Hathaway's Cottage
at Shottery near Stratford-upon-Avon.

**'Lillies of All Kinds'**

(*Iris pseudacorus* and *Lilium* sp.)

Perdita concludes her speech on spring flowers:

> Lillies of all kinds,
> The flower-de-luce being one. O, these I lack
> To make you garlands of.

Today flower-de-luce is identified with a wild iris of uncertain species — here portrayed as yellow flag. Formerly it was often considered a lily, with which garden favourites it is shown, but Lyte's *Herbal* of 1578 already makes the distinction.

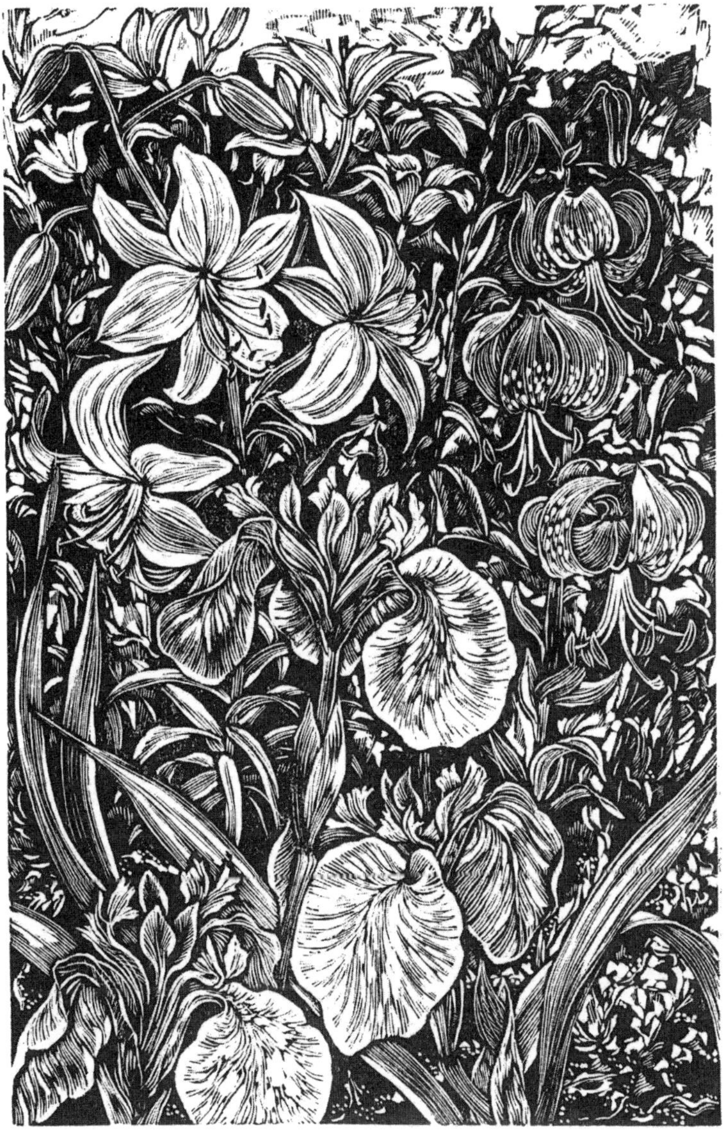

**White Lily** (*Lilium candidum*)

None of the many kinds of lilies found in England is a native wild flower. They were all introduced from different parts of the world, several before Shakespeare's time. Of these the stately, tall, white lily has been widely celebrated by poets for its elegance, beauty and purity. In Christian art it became a symbol of the Virgin Mary, and in literature, by inference, a standard compliment for any virgin a poet might wish to celebrate or flatter. So in Shakespeare's *Henry VIII*, Archbishop Cranmer predicts at the birth of Princess Elizabeth:

> yet a virgin,
> A most unspotted lily shall she pass
> To th' ground....
>
> 5.4.60–62

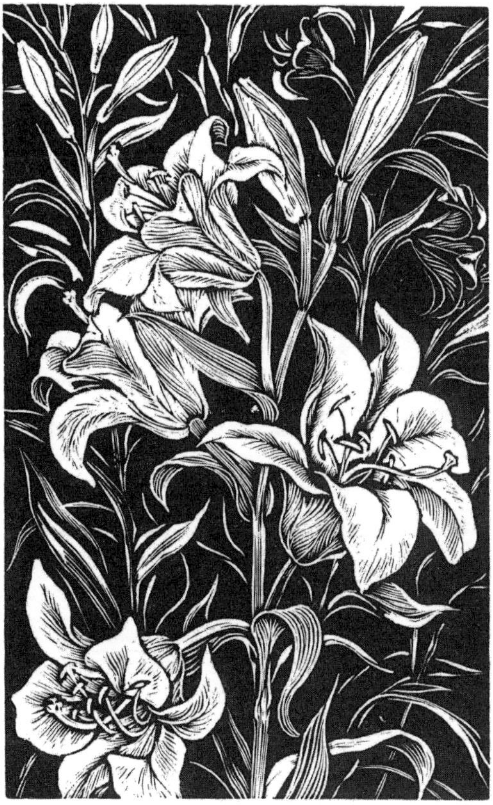

**Lily** (*Lilium* sp.)

While in many of Shakespeare's references one cannot be certain about the particular species he may have been alluding to, it is probable that, except in heraldic passages where 'lily' means flower-de-luce, he usually had the white or madonna lily in mind. It is the flower to which Queen Katharine compares herself when facing Cardinal Wolsey and her impending rejection by the King in *Henry VIII*:

> like the lily
> That once was mistress of the field, and flourished,
> I'll hang my head and perish.
>
> 3. 1. 151–153

As 'mistress of the field', the lily had only one rival, the rose. And so the beauty of an idealized person was conventionally described as a combination of white lily and red rose (with the lily only sometimes also standing for virtue), as in *Sonnet 98*, where the poet reflects about the absent young nobleman:

> Nor did I wonder at the lily's white,
> Nor praise the deep vermilion in the rose,
> They were but sweet, but figures of delight,
> Drawn after you, you pattern of all those.

In *King John*, Constance tells her son Arthur:

> Nature and fortune joined to make thee great:
> Of nature's gifts thou mayst with lilies boast
> And with the half-blown rose.
>
> 3. 1. 52–54

Another widely appreciated species was the scarlet chalcedonian lily. But the only possible allusion to it,

> A lily pale with damask die to grace her

in the seventh sonnet of *The Passionate Pilgrim*, is probably not by Shakespeare, and damask is the colour of carnations, not scarlet. Nor does Shakespeare refer to the other white but much smaller lily-of-the-valley. In Launce's mock-romantic description of his sister

> As white as a lily and as small as a wand
>
> *Two Gentlemen of Verona*, 2. 3. 20

'small' refers to the white lily's slender stem.

**Canker Rose** or **Dog Rose** (*Rosa canina*)

The largest of the English wild roses, it was often referred to as inferior to royal, cultivated roses. Shakespeare quibbles several times on the word 'canker', by which he means the canker worm, a caterpillar that gnaws the hearts of rose-buds:

> The canker-blooms have full as deep a dye
> As the perfumed tincture of the roses,
> …,
> But for their virtue only is their show,
> They live unwoo'd, and unrespected fade,
> Die to themselves.

Sonnet 54, 5–6, 9–11

Hotspur comments on Bolingbroke's usurpation of the throne as Henry IV when he deposed Richard II:

> To put down Richard, that sweet lovely rose,
> And plant this thorn, this canker, Bolingbroke.

*Henry IV, First Part,* 1. 3. 175–176

The morose Don John will not be reconciled to Don Pedro, his brother and prince:

> I had rather be a canker in a hedge than a rose in his grace.

*Much Ado about Nothing,* 1. 3. 27–28

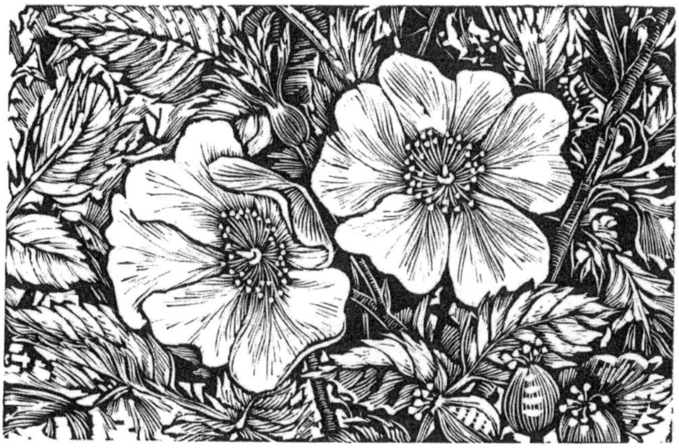

**Musk Rose** (*Rosa moschata*)

A rambling rose with large, white flowers of a musky fragrance, it was a great favourite in Shakespeare's time for its scent. Now less common, it is usually seen growing against the walls of old houses. It was introduced in England from southern Europe around 1540 and is shown here in the garden at Hall's Croft, the house occupied by Shakespeare's daughter, Susanna, and her husband, Dr John Hall.

Shakespeare's three references to the musk rose are all in *A Midsummer Night's Dream*. When Titania calls upon her train of diminutive fairies to engage in various activities, she asks some of them

> To kill cankers in the musk rose buds
>
> 2. 2. 3

Later, when Oberon has caused her ludicrously to dote upon Bottom, himself transformed into an ass, she invites him:

> Come sit thee down upon this flow'ry bed,
> While I thy amiable cheeks do coy
> And stick musk roses in thy sleek smooth head,
> And kiss thy fair large ears, my gentle joy.
>
> 4. 1. 1–4

---

*canker*: caterpillar; *coy*: caress

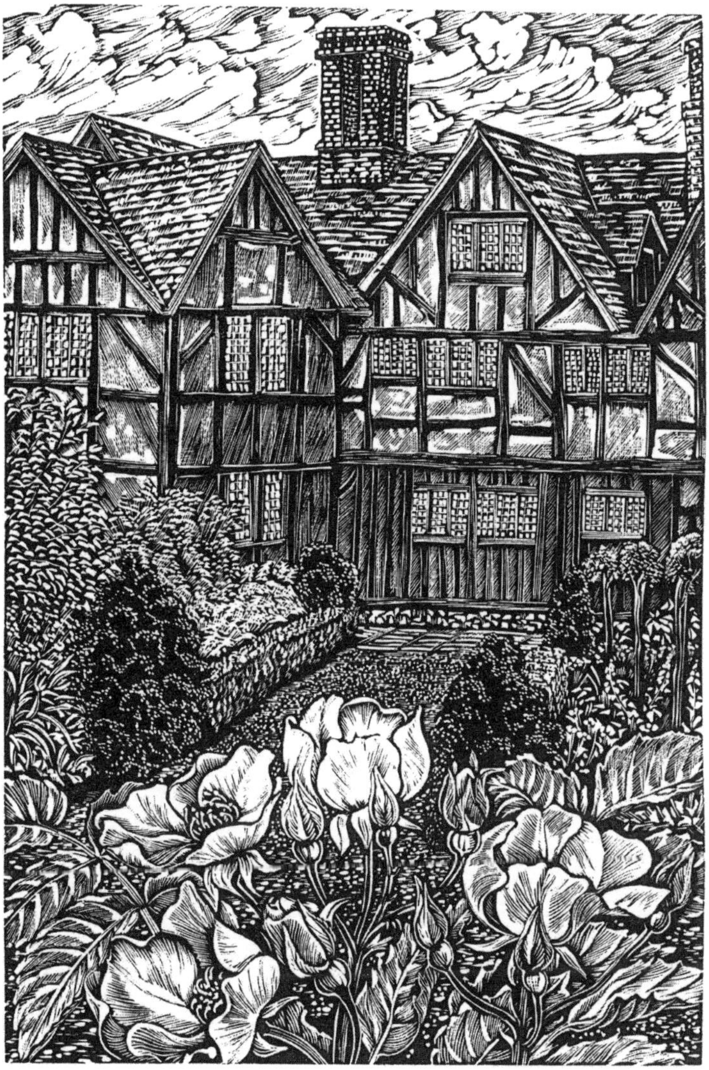

Musk roses at Hall's Croft Garden.

## **Damask Rose** (*Rosa damascena*)

As its name suggests, this favourite, ornamental, sweet-scented rose was introduced from Damascus. It is grown in many varieties. Among the wares Autolycus peddles at a country fair in Bohemia are

> Gloves as sweet as damask roses
>
> *The Winter's Tale*, 4. 4. 220

But in *Love's Labour's Lost*, a much earlier play, Boyet characteristically puns on the word:

> Fair ladies mask'd are roses in their bud;
> Dismask'd, their damask sweet commixture shown,
> Are angels vailing clouds, or roses blown.
>
> 5. 2. 295–297

---

*vailing*: letting fall the clouds that hid them; *blown*: in full bloom

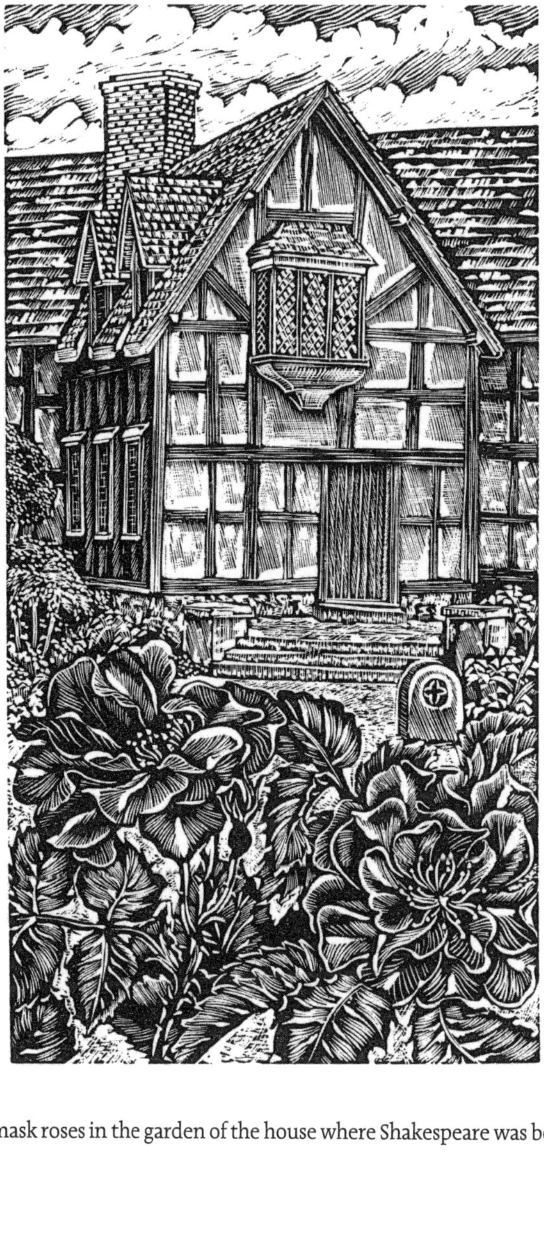

Damask roses in the garden of the house where Shakespeare was born.

**Provincial** or **Provençal Rose** (*Rosa provincialis* or *Rosa centifolia*)

Shakespeare's only allusion to this magnificent garden plant introduced from southern France is quite indirect. After the play-within-the-play in *Hamlet* has concluded with the tumultuous exit of the king, the highly excited prince asks his friend, Horatio, who has witnessed the scene:

> Would not this, sir, and a forest of feathers — if the rest of my fortunes turn Turk with me — with two Provincial roses on my razed shoes, get me a fellowship in a cry of players?
>
> 3. 2. 275–278

Congratulating himself for his own astute acting, Hamlet suggests that he would deserve a place in a professional acting company, especially if he had the plumes ('forest of feathers'), worn by tragic actors of his time, and their kinds of shoes, whose large rosettes concealed the ties.

---

*Turk with*: against; *cry*: company

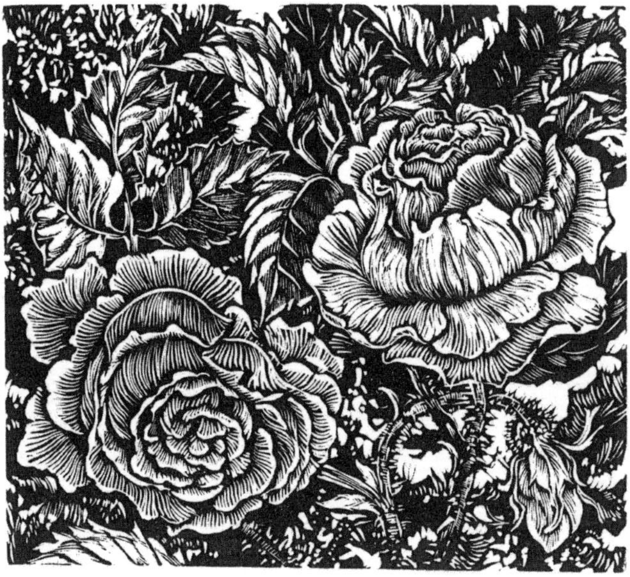

**Primrose, Harebell** and **Eglantine**

(*Primula vulgaris, Endymion non-scriptus* and *Rosa rubiginosa*)

thou shalt not lack
The flower that's like thy face, pale primrose, nor
The azur'd harebell, like thy veins: no, nor
The leaf of eglantine, whom not to slander,
Outsweet'ned not thy breath.

*Cymbeline*, 4. 2. 220–224

These lines are spoken by Arviragus, who with his brother is preparing the grave of Fidele (their unrecognized sister, Imogen) whom, because of the effect of a sleeping potion, they believe to have died. Perdita, too, speaks of 'pale primroses' in lines cited on page 66 that allude to the flower's blooming long before the sun reaches its height.

With its fragrant, blue-violet flowers in a one-sided spike, the harebell is a common flower of the woods during spring and early summer. It is better known today as bluebell or wild hyacinth, and by at least three different Latin (scientific) names: *Hyacinthoides non-scripta, Scilla non-scripta* and *Endymion non-scriptus*.

Eglantine or sweet-briar is a small, thorny shrub, valued chiefly for its very sweet-scented leaves, though it can hurt ('prick') as well as give pleasure. For Oberon's allusion to it, see page 22.

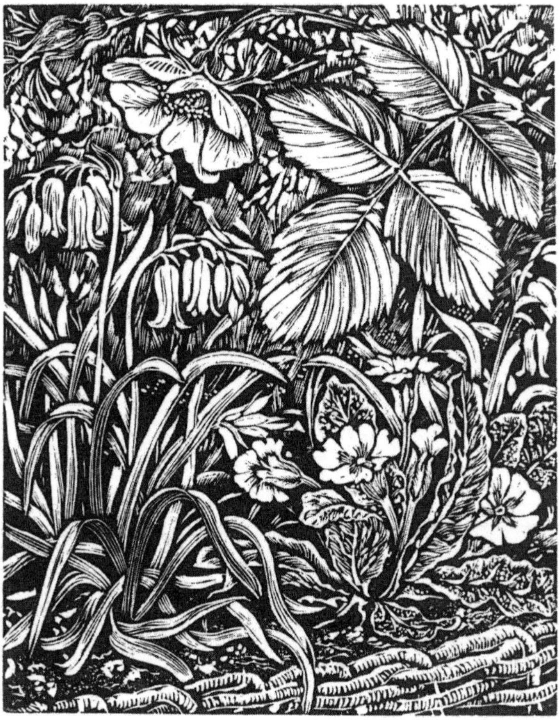

## **Common Mallow** (*Malva sylvestris*)

The context of Shakespeare's only reference to mallows shows that he was thinking of the common roadside weed. When, after the storm with which *The Tempest* opens, the shipwrecked royal party find themselves wandering on the island and King Alonso is despondent in the belief that his son Ferdinand has drowned, Gonzalo tries to distract and cheer his master with a fanciful description of the utopian commonwealth he would create on the island if he could be its master. However, two of his evil companions (Prospero's brother, Antonio, who usurped his throne in Milan, and Alonso's brother, Sebastian) interrupt his fancy with cynical comments:

> Antonio: He'd sow't with nettle-seed.
> Sebastian: Or docks, or mallows.
>
> 2. 1. 144–145

Of these weeds, mallows are clearly the most handsome, since these sprawling, coarse and hairy perennials, up to three feet in height, are graced with large, attractive pink flowers, their petals lined with darker veins. This, however, was obviously not in Sebastian's mind.

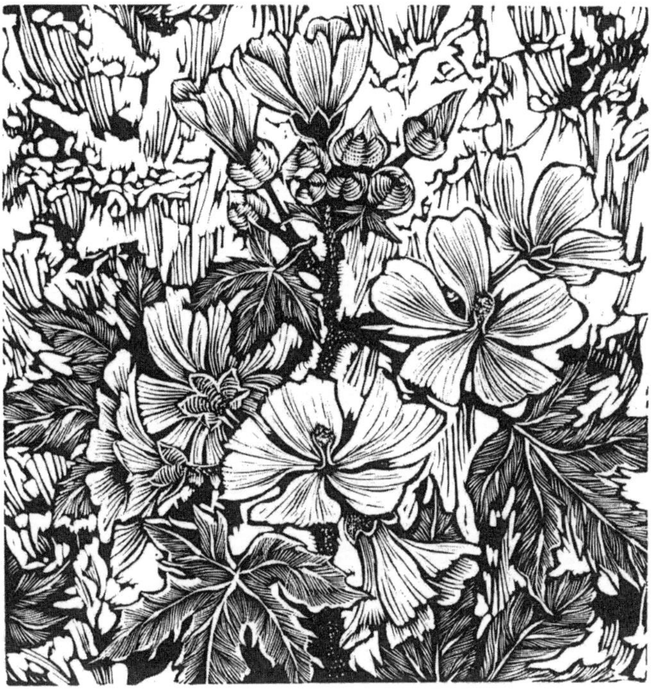

**Eringo** or **Sea-holly** (*Eryngium maritimum*)

Shakespeare's single reference is not to the plant itself, but to the candied roots of the sea-holly, then a well-known aphrodisiac, for which Gerard in his famous *Herbal* of 1597 provides a recipe.

The plant is so called because it is usually found growing on sand by the sea, and because its spiny leaves resemble those of holly. The plant's silvery-blue cast and blue-mauve flowerheads are striking and distinctive.

Near the end of *The Merry Wives of Windsor,* Falstaff is tricked by Mistress Page and Mistress Ford into believing that, if in Windsor forest he ridiculously dons a buck's head, they will meet him there and respond to his advances. It is when they appear and Mistress Ford briefly allows him to embrace her that he exultantly exclaims:

> My doe with the black scut? Let the sky rain potatoes ...
> and snow eringoes; let there come a tempest of provocation,
> I will shelter me here.
>
> 5.5.18–21

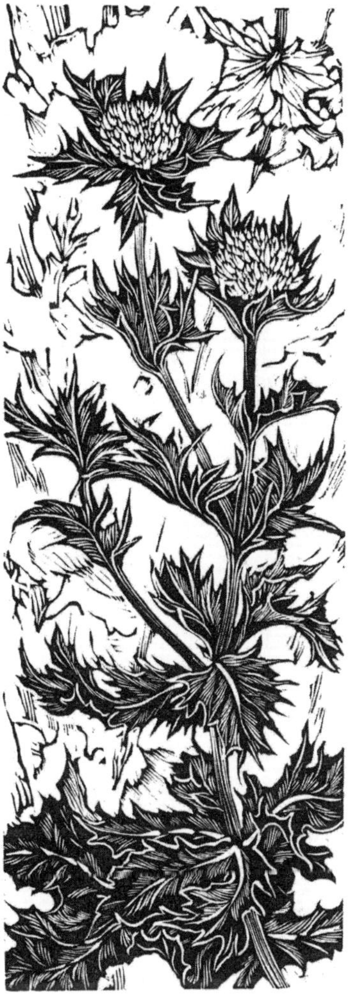

## Flowers for a Bride and Bridegroom

No other passage in Shakespeare refers to as many flowers as the boy's song at the beginning of *The Two Noble Kinsmen,* a play on which Shakespeare late in his life collaborated with Fletcher. The scene opens with an elaborate ceremony of Duke Theseus's wedding to Hippolyta. The opening stage direction begins:

> *Music. Enter Hymen with a torch burning; a boy in a white robe before, singing and strewing flowers.*
>
> Roses, their sharp spines being gone,
> Not royal in their smells alone,
>     But in their hue;
> Maiden pinks, of odour faint,
> Daisies smell-less, yet most quaint,
>     And sweet thyme true.
>
> 1.1.1–6

Each of the four flowers included in the first stanza is appropriate for the wedding ceremony. The rose was associated with royalty and with Venus, goddess of beauty and love; daisies with innocence; thyme (lower right) with truth and faithfulness; and maiden pink (*Dianthus deltoides*), here shown in the upper left, with purity and virginity. This sprawling, greyish perennial with freckled pink, toothed petals is found in sunny gardens as well as dry wild places.

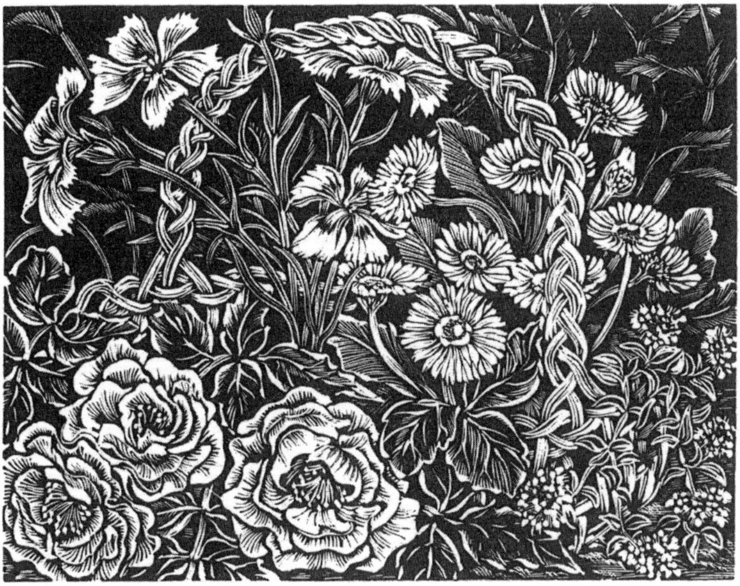

Clockwise from lower left: roses, pinks, daisies and thyme.
(*Rosa* sp., *Dianthus deltoides, Bellis perennis* and *Thymus vulgaris.*)

The boy's song continues:

Primrose, first-born child of ver,
Merry springtime's harbinger
    with harebells dim;
Oxlips, in their cradles growing,
Marigolds, on death-beds blowing,
    Lark's-heels trim;

All dear nature's children sweet,
Lie 'fore bride and bridegroom's feet,
    Blessing their sense.
(*he strews flowers*)

These flowers too are appropriate for the marriage ritual. The primrose as an early spring flower stands for cheerfulness and fertility; the harebell (or bluebell) signifies good fortune and protection against evil; and marigolds are an emblem of constant affection.

This is Shakespeare's only reference to lark's heel. Also called larkspur or garden delphinium (*Delphinium ajacis*), this fairly tall and popular garden plant native to the Mediterranean had by then been extensively naturalized in England.

---

*ver*: spring, in Latin

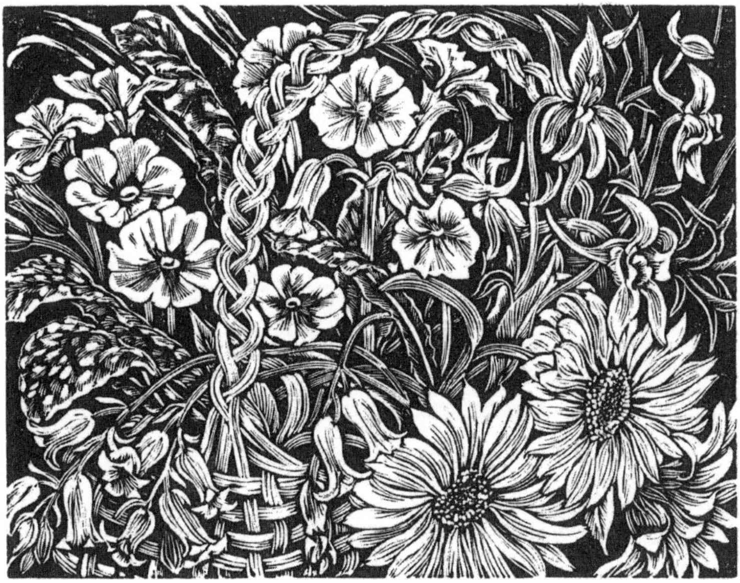

Clockwise from lower left: harebell, primrose, oxlip, lark's heel and marigold.
(*Endymion non-scriptus, Primula vulgaris, Primula elatior, Delphinium ajacis* and *Calendula officinalis.*)

## **Herb of Grace** or **Rue** (*Ruta graveolens*)

Rue is an evergreen shrub native to southern Europe, with bitter, strong-scented leaves, that was introduced into English herb gardens as a kind of heal-all early in the Middle Ages. Today it is often seen in rock gardens.

It is frequently alluded to, often punningly, by Elizabethan poets, who liked playing on the association of the bitter-leaved rue with 'rue' or repentance and 'ruth' or pity, as in these lines by the Gardener in *Richard II*, referring to Richard's Queen, who is grieving her separation from her husband who is about to be deposed:

> Here did she fall a tear, here in this place
> I'll set a bank of rue, sour herb of grace.
> Rue, even for ruth, here shortly shall be seen
> In the remembrance of a weeping queen.
>
> 3.4.104–107

Ophelia in *Hamlet* says of rue:

> We may call it herb of grace a' Sundays
>
> 4.5.182–183

This other name evidently developed from the herb's link with repentance that is bestowed by divine grace. When, in *Antony and Cleopatra*, on the evening before the battle with Octavius, Antony speaks to his followers with melancholy foreboding, and Enobarbus chides him for making them weep, he pulls himself together with words that recall those of the Gardener:

> Grace grow where those drops fall, my hearty friends
>
> 4.2.38

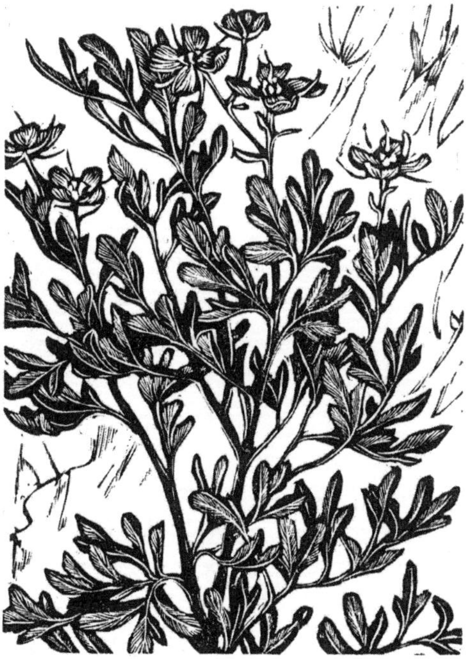

**Ophelia Bestowing Flowers:**
**Rosemary** and **Pansy** (*Rosmarinus officinalis* and *Viola tricolor*)

> Ophelia (*to Laertes*): There's rosemary, that's for remembrance; pray you, love, remember. And there's pansies, that's for thoughts.
>
> Laertes: A document in madness, thoughts and remembrance fitted.
>
> Ophelia (*to Gertrude*): There's fennel for you, and columbines. (*to Claudius*): There's rue for you, and here's some for me; we may call it herb of grace a' Sundays. You may wear your rue with a difference. There's a daisy. I would give you some violets, but they withered all when my father died.
>
> *Hamlet*, 4. 5. 175–185

In this famous episode, the mad Ophelia is handing different flowers to her brother Laertes, the queen, and the king. She bestows rosemary and pansies upon Laertes whom, however, she appears to confuse with Hamlet. In art and literature, both flowers symbolized remembrance, especially that of the giver. For this, see also the reference to Ophelia on page 42 and Friar Laurence's urging of Juliet's passionately grieving parents:

> Dry up your tears, and stick your rosemary
> On this fair corse.
>
> *Romeo and Juliet*, 4. 5. 79–80

The name pansy or 'pawnce' was derived from the French *pensée*. Elsewhere Shakespeare calls it love-in-idleness, shown on page 21, which had a quite different association.

---

*document in madness*: lesson in this mad talk; *with a difference*: for a different kind of sorrow

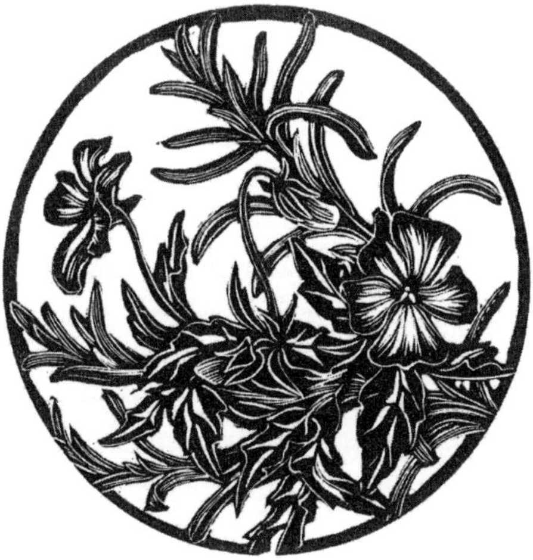

**Columbine** and **Fennel**
(*Aquilegia vulgaris* and *Foeniculum vulgare*)

Shakespeare probably intended each flower to be suitably fitted in its symbolic meaning to its recipient, who presumably is meant to take it to the undecked grave of Ophelia's father; but the earliest surviving texts of *Hamlet* are without stage directions, and modern scholars are uncertain as to which flowers are intended for the king and queen. Here we interpret that Ophelia presents fennel, which stands for flattery, and columbines, whose horned nectaries suggest cuckoldry, to Gertrude; and that rue, also known as herb of grace (see page 96), is meant for the king with his guilty conscience as well as for herself, but with a 'difference'. The daisy suggests Ophelia's own innocence and her love, but it is not clear to whom she gives it. For violets and their association with death and Ophelia, see page 16. They withered, as Ophelia tells us, when Polonius dies.

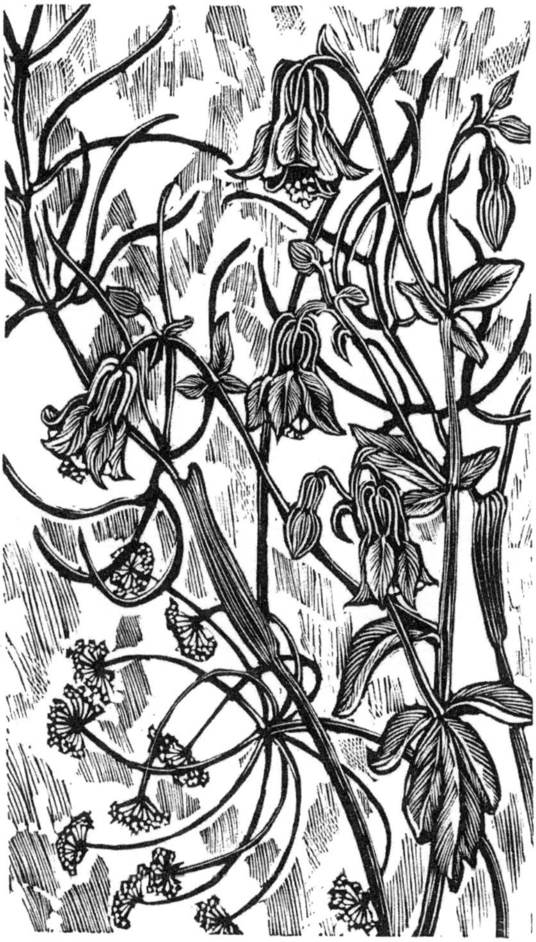

## **Broom** (*Cytisus scoparius*)

This shrub with its many branches, beautiful, large, golden-yellow flowers and fragrance was a favourite in England and Scotland as well as France long before Shakespeare. Broom had moreover been originally associated with the long-ruling dynasty of the Plantagenets in England, who were descendants of Geoffrey, Count of Anjou; since he liked wearing a sprig of broom in his cap, Geoffrey was nicknamed after its contemporary Latin name, *Planta genista.*

Several poets thus have celebrated the plant for its beauty. But not Shakespeare. Broom can grow so high as to justify Iris's lines in the masque in *The Tempest,*

> and thy broom groves
> Whose shadow the dismissed bachelor loves,
> Being lass-lorn.
>
> 4.1.66–68

but that is Shakespeare's only reference to the plant itself. In two others he refers to the brooms made from it.

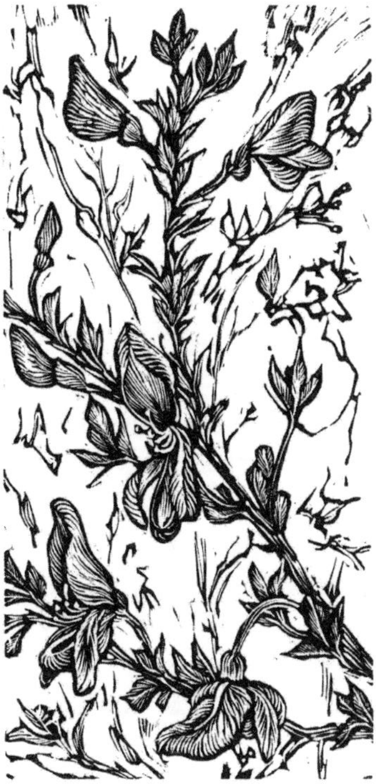

## **Cultivated Flax** (*Linum usitatissimum*)

England's flora includes three native flaxes, the smallest of which, the fairy flax, Ellacombe calls 'one of the most graceful ornaments of our higher downs and hills'. Many species of flaxes have been cultivated as ornamental garden plants. But the seven times Shakespeare mentions flax, he clearly has the flax of commerce in mind, which had early been introduced to England from Egypt. Shakespeare surely knew the delight of seeing a crop of flax like a vast sheet of pure, bright blue. The flowers, almost an inch across, rest on dainty stalks with narrow, lanceolate, three-veined leaves.

Shakespeare, however, usually refers to the spinning of flax or spun flax which in his time was an occupation of women in every household, poor or rich. So Sir Toby in *Twelfth Night* jokes bawdily about Sir Andrew Aguecheek's flock of hair:

> It hangs like flax on a distaff; and I hope to see a housewife take
> thee between her legs, and spin it off.
>
> 1. 3. 102–104

Linseed oil and linseed meal were made from the seeds of the plant, and still another use was in first aid. In *King Lear*, a servant coming to the cruelly blinded Gloucester's aid, tells his fellows:

> I'll fetch some flax and whites of eggs
> To apply to his bleeding face. Now heaven help him!
>
> 3. 7. 106–107

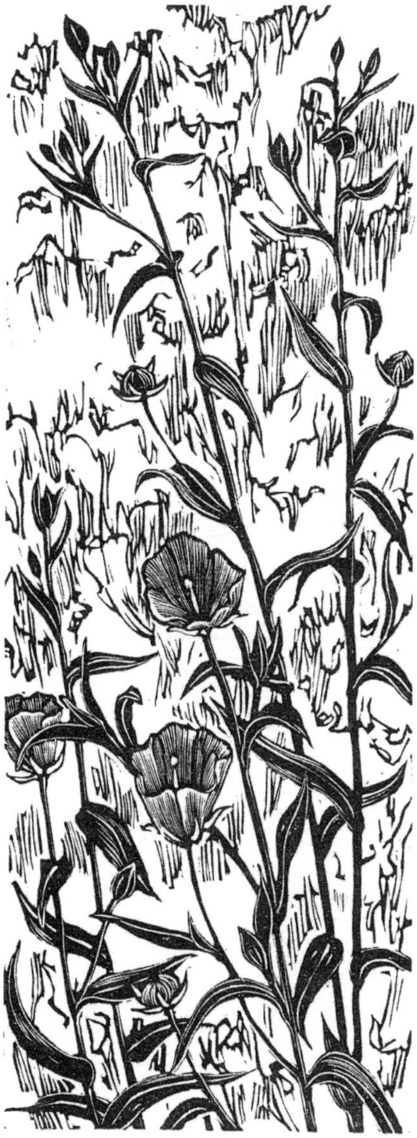

**Daisy** (*Bellis perennis*)

Two centuries before Shakespeare, the poet Chaucer explained the etymology of the familiar flower's name in *The Dayeseye, or Ellis the Eye of Day;* its little flowerheads with yellow disc and white or pink rays open in the morning and close at night. In his still instructive *The Plant-lore and Garden-craft of Shakespeare,* Ellacombe includes an essay on the daisy in legend and poetry. Several lyrical poets of Shakespeare's time celebrated the 'daisy delectable'.

In High Renaissance paintings of the adoration, the daisy is a symbol of the innocence of the Christ Child. None of Shakespeare's references to the daisy has such a direct religious meaning, but Ophelia's fondness for it suits her own innocence: it is one of the flowers she carries in her mad scene (see page 98) and it forms part of the 'fantastic garlands' the Queen describes her as wearing when she fell to her death into a stream (pages 42 and 44).

Like Ophelia, Imogen in *Cymbeline* is both fond of flowers and innocent. But the episode where she grieves over the headless Cloten, her boorish enemy, is grotesquely ironic because she mistakes his body for that of her husband, Posthumus. Yet when Lucius, the Roman general, comes upon the pathetic scene, he responds with a movingly poetic command:

> ... let us
> Find out the prettiest daisied plot we can,
> And make him with our pikes and partisans
> A grave.
>
> 4. 2. 397–400

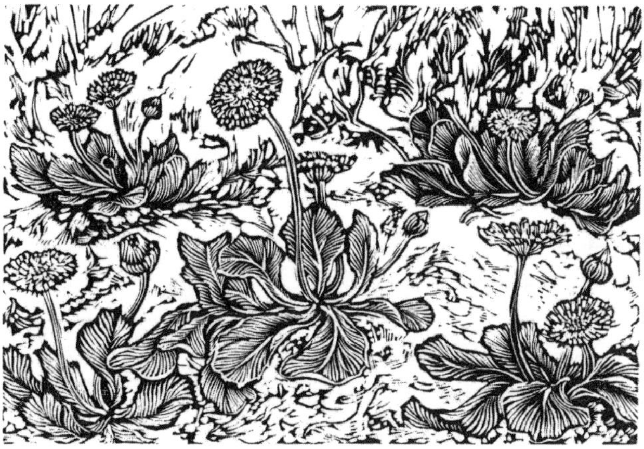

**Rank and Idle Weeds:**
**Fumitory** and **Perennial Rye-grass** (*Fumaria officinalis* and *Lolium perenne*)

There are two passages, in *Henry V*, and in *King Lear*, where Shakespeare refers to a similar cluster of 'idle' or 'hateful' weeds mixed with one or more attractive wild flowers. So many of the plants in the two passages are moreover identical that, though the contexts are very different, the lines in *King Lear* echo those Shakespeare wrote earlier for the Duke of Burgundy's speech in *Henry V*. In *King Lear*, the lines spoken by Cordelia describe how her mad father, wandering alone on the heath and 'singing aloud', has crowned himself grotesquely:

> ... with rank fumiter and furrow-weeds,
> with hardocks, hemlock, nettles, cuckoo-flowers
> darnel, and all the idle weeds that grow
> in our sustaining corn.
>
> 4.4.3–6

Coming as he did from a small town, Shakespeare knew that darnel, fumitory and hemlock commonly grow together on neglected land and in farmyards. In our time, darnel or rye-grass (various species of *Lolium*) is being cultivated. But there is no use for fumiter or fumitory, a plentiful weed of spreading or clambering habit and with pinkish-purple to creamy white flowers in spikes. (Shakespeare mentions lady-smocks, another name for cuckoo-flower, in the song of spring near the end of *Love's Labour's Lost*, cited and pictured on pages 32, 33. For nettles see pages 124, 125.)

---

*hardocks*: burdocks

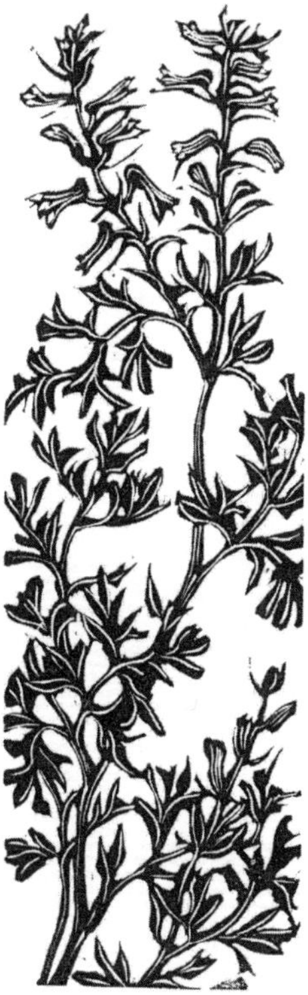

Fumitory

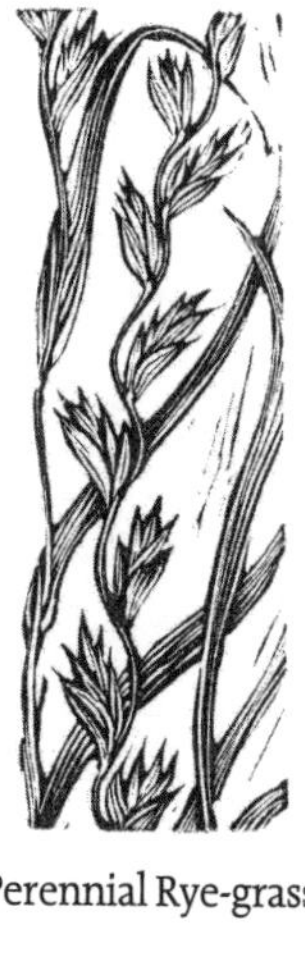

Perennial Rye-grass

**Hemlock** (*Conium maculatum*)

Hemlock (not to be confused with the evergreen tree that also bears this name) is a tall, white-flowered umbellifer with hollow, purple-flecked stems. Its blooms are a familiar sight in hedgerows, on roadsides and on waste ground in mid-summer. Its stem has an unpleasant smell when bruised. Its juice, fruit and leaves are poisonous and it is believed that it was with this juice that Socrates was put to death.

It is therefore a fitting ingredient of the witches' brew in *Macbeth*:

> Scale of dragon, tooth of wolf
> Witch's mummy, maw and gulf
> Of the ravin'd salt-sea shark,
> Root of hemlock digg'd i' th' dark,

4. 1. 22–25

But in *King Lear* (see previous page), the following speech by Burgundy, and elsewhere, Shakespeare simply associates hemlock with other weeds.

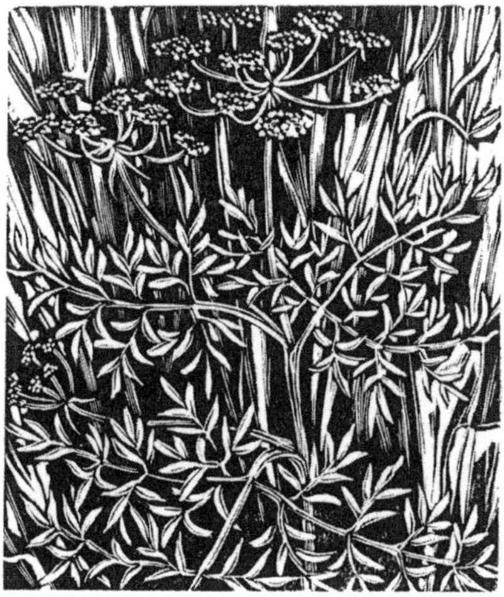

## **Great Burdock** (*Arctium lappa*)

Burgundy's lines form part of a speech early in the last scene of *Henry V*. After the defeat of the French by Henry's forces at Agincourt, he has called together the kings of Britain and France, accompanied by dukes with their ladies, for a peace conference. In a long and moving plea for peace, he vividly describes the effects of war on the neglected countryside of 'our fertile France':

> ... her fallow leas
> The darnel, hemlock and rank fumitory
> Doth root upon, while that the coulter rusts
> That should deracinate such savagery;
> The even mead, that erst brought sweetly forth
> The freckled cowslip, burnet, and green clover,
> Wanting the scythe withal, uncorrected, rank,
> Conceives by idleness, and nothing teems
> But hateful docks, rough thistles, kecksies, burrs
> Losing both beauty and utility.
>
> 5.2.44–53

The 'burrs' Burgundy includes in his catalogue of weeds are those with clinging seeds, such as the great burdock shown here.

---

*lea*: tract of open, here agricultural, land; *rank*: over-abundant; *coulter*: iron blade fixed in front of a plough; *deracinate*: uproot; *even mead*: level meadow; *wanting*: lacking; *teems*: is born

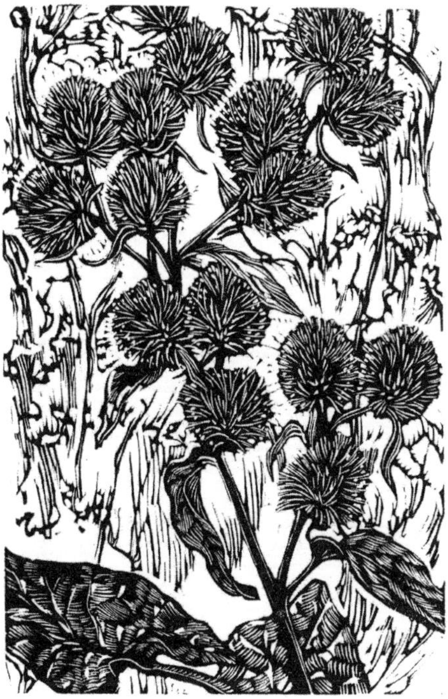

**Salad Burnet, Cowslips** and **Green Clover**
(*Poterium sanguisorba, Primula veris* and *Trifolium repens*)

Burgundy's speech on the previous page includes three plants of meadow and wayside that represent a healthy, well-tended landscape which symbolizes a peaceful, well-governed country.

Salad burnet (seen here on the upper left), with its pinnate leaves and flowering stalk, smells of cucumber when crushed. An unassuming plant, it grows about a foot high with its tiny flowers in globular heads coloured by yellow stamens. It is shown here with freckled or spotted cowslips (on the right), with their inflated calyces or whorls of joined sepals and their often drooping flowers. On the lower left is clover with its clustered flowers and trefoil leaves.

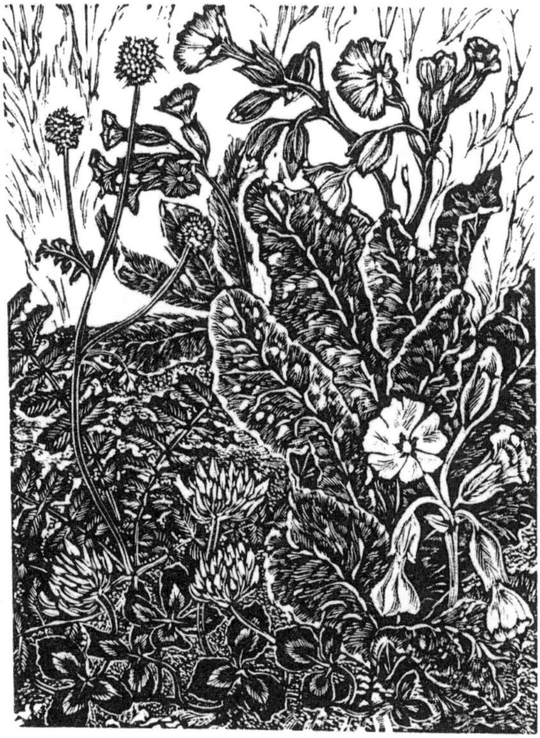

Clockwise from upper left: Salad Burnet, Cowslips and Green Clover.

**Kecksies**

'Kecksies' or 'kecks', as they are usually called today, include several of the *Umbelliferae* group of plants, including cow parsley, chervil and more. Here they are shown growing near the ruins of Kenilworth Castle in Warwickshire, the Earl of Leicester's country-seat not far from Stratford, where Queen Elizabeth and her court were sometimes feasted with elaborate entertainments.

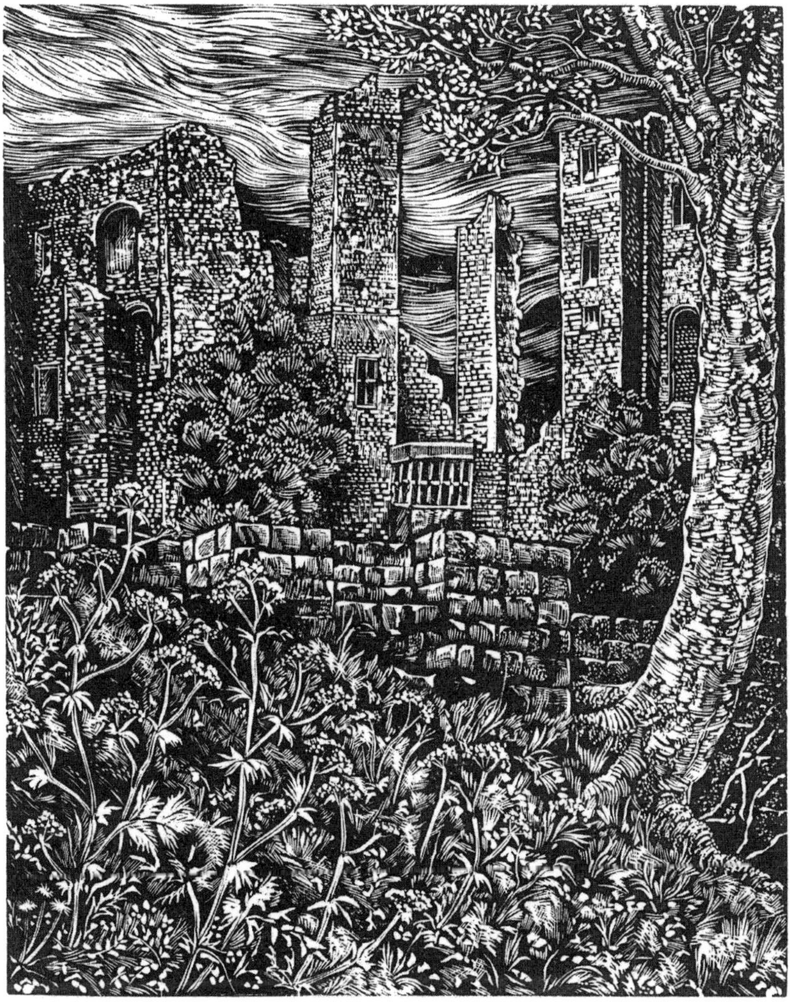

**Hawthorn** (*Crataegus monogyna*)

Hawthorn is a familiar thorny shrub with deeply lobed leaves and clusters of white, strongly scented flowers. It is commonly found growing in hedgerows, as the original meaning of 'haw' reflects. Poets often associated it with an idyllic countryside, where resting shepherds enjoy its sweet fragrance and shade. Thus Shakespeare's troubled King Henry VI wonders:

> Gives not the hawthorn bush a sweeter shade
> To shepherds looking on their silly sheep
> Than doth a rich embroider'd canopy
> To kings that fear their subjects' treachery?
>
> *Henry VI, Third Part,* 2. 5. 42–45

The bird sitting on the hawthorn branch is an English or European robin, a much-loved bird common in both towns and countryside.

The older name, 'ruddock', which Shakespeare uses in *Cymbeline* (act 4, sc. 2), conveys its colour more accurately than the familiar 'robin redbreast'. Shakespeare alludes to its insistent, flute-like song in *The Two Gentlemen of Verona,* when Valentine's servant, Speed, surprises his master by telling him that he knows he is in love from typical symptoms. Valentine used to

> crow like a cock

whenever he was laughing, but now relishes

> a love-song, like a robin-redbreast.
>
> 2. 1. 20–27

---

*silly*: simple

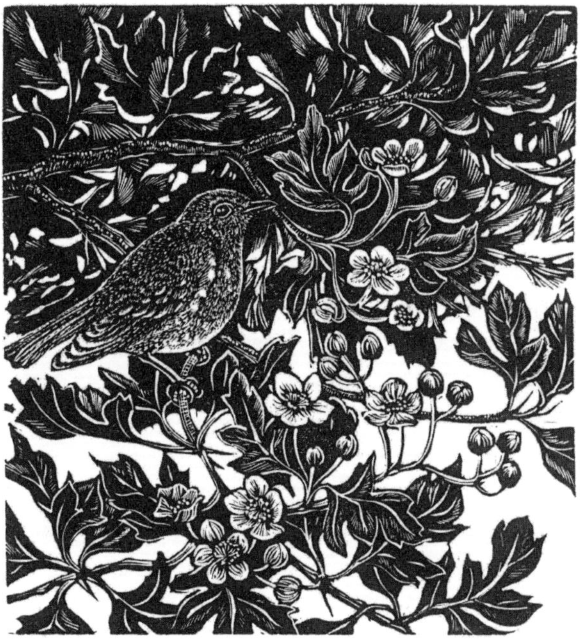

**Saffron** or **Autumn Crocus** (*Crocus sativus*)

This plant was introduced to Europe, including England, from the Near East during the Middle Ages. Its purple flowers bloom in late autumn. The flowers of meadow saffron *Colchicum autumnale*, which confusingly is also called 'autumn crocus', are rosy-mauve by contrast.

In Shakespeare's time, varieties of saffron crocus were cultivated especially in Cambridgeshire and around Saffron Walden for the orange-yellow dye that was made from the dried stigmas and part of the style of the flower, and it was also used for flavouring as well as colouring sauces and pastry.

In *All's Well That Ends Well*, Lord Lafeu comments scornfully on how the comic braggart, Monsieur Parolles, apes the courtly fashion by wearing

> villainous saffron
>
> 4.5.2

that is, a starched ruff yellow with saffron. In *The Winter's Tale*, the clown includes

> saffron to colour the warden pies
>
> 4.3.45–46

— that is, pies made of cooking pears — in the list of supplies he needs to buy for the sheep-shearing festival in pastoral Bohemia.

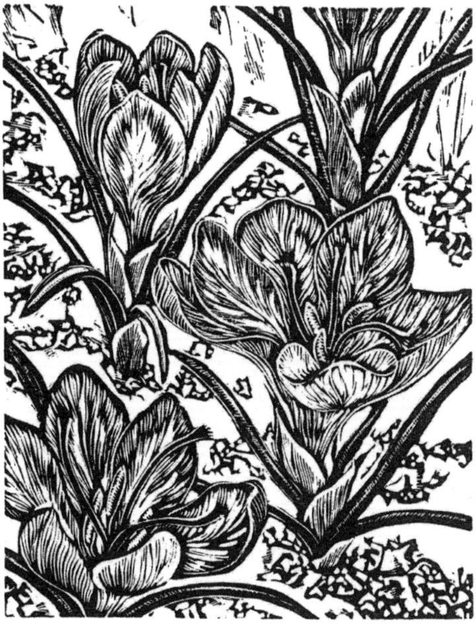

## **Monkshood** (*Aconitum napellus*)

Introduced as early as the tenth century, different species of aconitum have been favourite ornamental plants in English gardens, especially *Aconitum napellus* with 'its stately habit and its handsome leaves' (Ellacombe's phrase) and beautiful blue flowers. But be on your guard, for all of the plant's parts, from its root to its pollen dust, are poisonous. It came to be called 'wolfsbane' because in early times wolves were hunted with arrows poisoned with the sap of aconitum.

So in Shakespeare's single allusion in *Henry IV, Second Part*, aconitum is representative of a violent poison. King Henry, after having advised his youngest son, Thomas of Clarence, on his deathbed how to conduct himself towards his brothers and especially Prince Hal, concludes:

> Learn this, Thomas,
> And thou shalt prove a shelter to thy friends,
> A hoop of gold to bind thy brothers in,
> That the united vessel of their blood,
> Mingled with venom of suggestion —
> As, force perforce, the age will pour it in —
> Shall never leak, though it do work as strong
> As aconitum or rash gunpowder.
>
> 4. 4. 41–48

Several images are combined in this passage: the barrel that unites the blood of the royal brothers, bound by a hoop of gold, will not leak, even if poisonous instigation to evil were to act on it as powerfully as aconitum or gunpowder.

That aconitum was not only used for nefarious ends but also believed to be an antidote against other poisons, is referred to in *Sejanus*, a play by Shakespeare's contemporary, Ben Jonson:

> I have heard that aconite,
> Being timely taken, hath a healing might
> Against the scorpion's stroke.
>
> 3. 3. 29–31

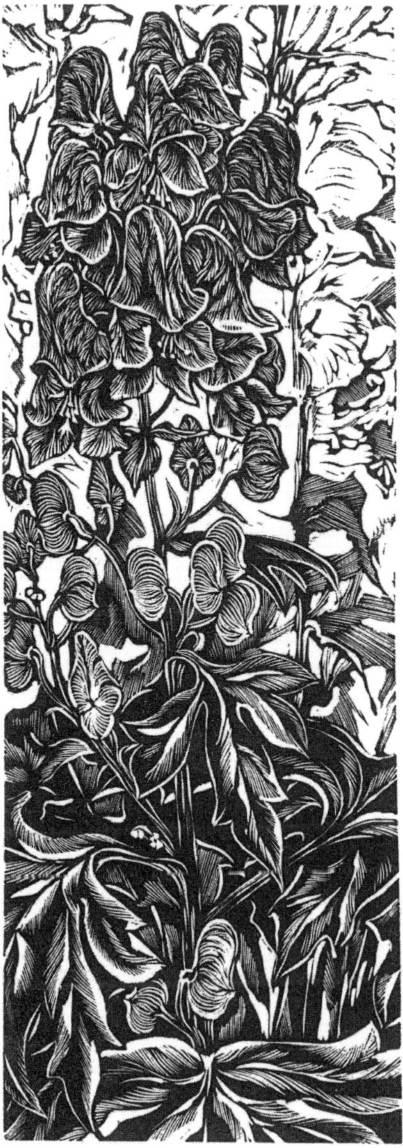

**Strawberry** under **Nettles** (*Fragaria vesca* and *Urtica dioica*)

In the opening scene of *Henry V* the Bishop of Ely uses the following image while discussing with the Archbishop of Canterbury Hal's miraculous-seeming and sudden transformation from an irresponsible playboy prince who liked associating with low company to an impressively mature and committed king:

> The strawberry grows underneath the nettle,
> And wholesome berries thrive and ripen best
> Neighbour'd by fruit of baser quality.
>
> 1. 1. 60–62

That Shakespeare is referring to the wild strawberry is probable because in his time they were gathered in woods and planted in gardens. They commonly grew underneath nettles, as shown in this engraving.

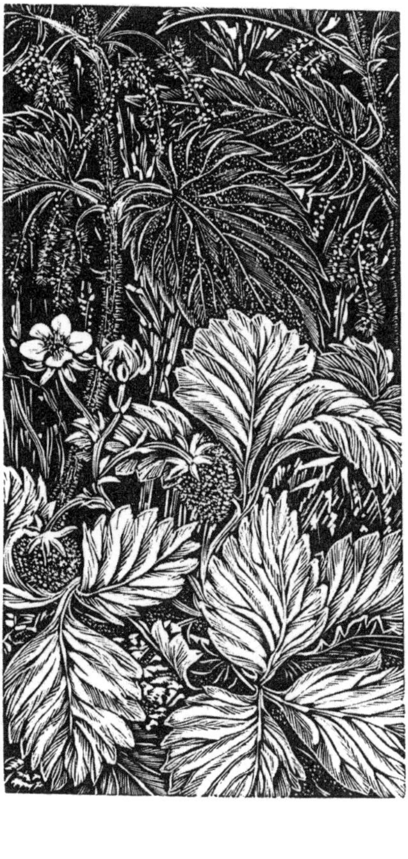

**Wormwood** (*Artemisia absinthium*)

This attractive and fairly common plant is seen growing in midsummer on wastelands and roadsides. It is smaller and more aromatic than the abundant mugwort (*Artemisia vulgaris*). Its distinctive marks are its grey foliage, branched spikes with numerous small, drooping, yellow flowerheads, and the fact that both stems and leaves are covered with a silky down.

Wormwood had a high medical reputation during the Middle Ages. It was thought to be beneficial for both heart and brain. It was also widely used as an insect repellent, especially against fleas, because of its extreme bitterness. Shakespeare alludes to two aspects of its bitterness; to the proverbial in Hamlet's famous aside,

> That's wormwood!
>
> *Hamlet*, 3. 2. 181

during the play-within-the-play, when the Player Queen protests to her husband that she would be 'accurst' if she ever married another man; and to the actual taste in the Nurse's hilarious though insensitive account in *Romeo and Juliet* how she weaned the baby Juliet from her breast:

> For I had then laid wormwood to my dug,
> ...
> When it did taste the wormwood on the nipple
> Of my dug and felt it bitter, pretty fool,
> To see it teachy and fall out wi' th' dug!
>
> 1. 3. 26, 30–32

---

*teachy*: tetchy, fretful

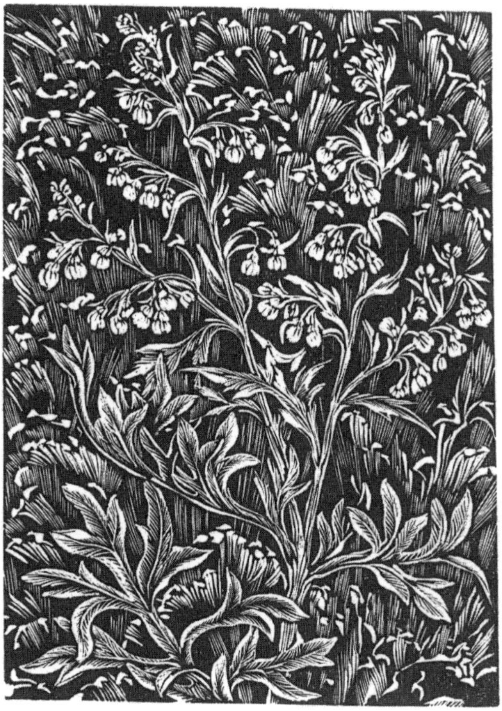

**Vetch** (*Vicia sativa*)

In the betrothal masque in *The Tempest* Iris, acting as Juno's messenger, calls upon Ceres, the goddess of vegetation, to leave her

> ... rich leas
> Of wheat, rye, barley, vetches, oats and pease.
>
> 4. 1. 60–61

Though there are several kinds of vetch that beautify English lanes and hedges with their purple flowers, this passage clearly alludes to the fodder plant known as cultivated or common vetch.

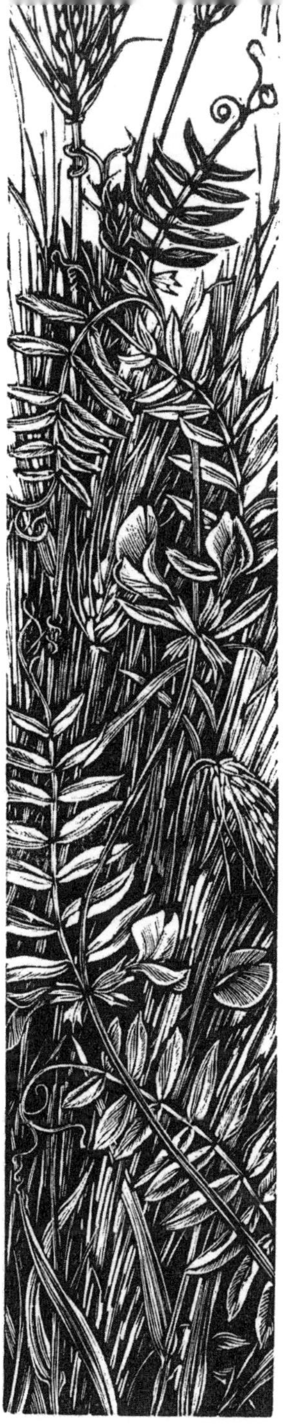

**Plantain**, probably **Ratstail Plantain**
(*Plantago major*)

The stoutest and coarsest of the plantains growing in England, common in farmyards, bare waste places, and also on lawns. Its large, broad, oval leaves had a high medical reputation, and Shakespeare's three references relate to its use as a home remedy for a grazed or 'broken' shin, as in Costard's clamour to Armado, rejecting more sophisticated medicines:

> O sir, plantain, a plain plantain; no l'envoi, no salve,
> sir, but a plantain!
>
> *Love's Labour's Lost*, 3. 1. 73–74

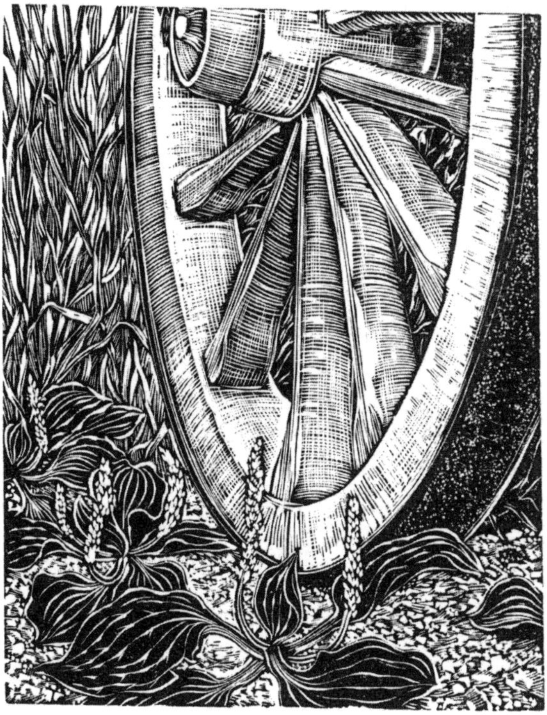

# Index



---

This index includes plants not mentioned by Shakespeare but included in the text.

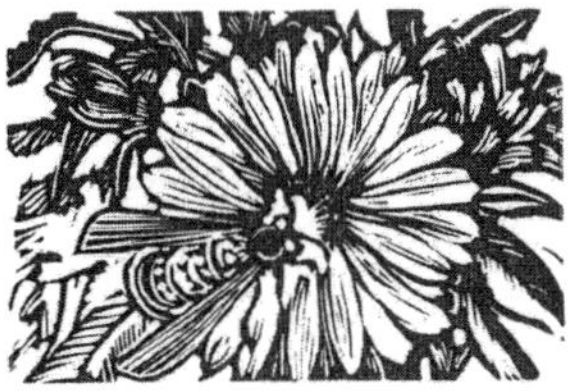

## Acknowledgements

A hand-crafted edition of ninety-seven copies of this work was originally published by Gerard Brender à Brandis in 1997. The engravings were printed from the endgrain, wooden blocks and the text from hand-set Libra type using an 1882 Albion printing press.

Thanks to Dorothy and Brian Parker for bringing together the Shakespearean scholar and the artist that made this project possible. We are grateful to the following for their support: Roger Pringle, Director of the Shakespeare Centre, Stratford-upon-Avon, and his staff; the Cambridge Botanic Garden, Cambridge, England; the Royal Botanical Gardens, Hamilton; and the University of Guelph. Also thanks to Marianne Brandis for her editorial expertise and advice.

We are indebted to Tim and Elke Inkster of the Porcupine's Quill for having published this new edition of our work, an edition which makes it available to a much larger audience than was possible with the original letterpress edition. Artists rarely receive the respect and craftsmanship which the Inksters bring to their publications.

Gerard Brender à Brandis is a member of the Society of Wood Engravers (England). He has produced hundreds of drawings, wood engravings and watercolours of flowering plants, many of which were studied in his own garden. These images have appeared in books, including *Wood, Ink and Paper* (1980), *Portraits of Flowers* (1995), and *An Artist's Garden* (2001), all published by The Porcupine's Quill, as well as in his own handmade editions. These have been included in the collections of the National Library (Ottawa), the New York Public Library, the National Library of New Zealand, and many public and university libraries as well as private collections. His single-leaf engravings are in the National Gallery (Ottawa), the Royal Botanical Gardens (Hamilton), the Missouri Botanic Garden, the Arnold Arboretum and the Hunt Botanical Library. His garden and his studio are located in Stratford, Ontario.

F. David Hoeniger is professor emeritus from Victoria College, University of Toronto, where he taught for many years in the Department of English. He is also a former director of the university's Centre for Reformation and Renaissance Studies. Professor Hoeniger is the author and editor of numerous works on Shakespeare, his work and his times, including *Medicine and Shakespeare in the English Renaissance* (1992), and *Science and the Arts in the Renaissance* (edited with John W. Shirley, 1985). His editions of Shakespeare include the Arden *Pericles* (1963) and *King Henry the Eighth* in *The Pelican Shakespeare* (1966). Professor Hoeniger lives in Toronto.

Finis